The Ultimate Guide to Avoiding Business Start-Up Failure

JOHN CHARMAN

DEDICATION

This book is dedicated to Friedrich A. Hayek, author of the *Road to Serfdom*. His life work, as an economist and philosopher, strengthened free markets and led to the foundation of libertarianism in the United States. He inspired Margaret Thatcher in her efforts to reverse nationalization and the restraints that central planning places on growth. May we remain vigilant in defense of the market economy; the most effective means of setting prices and releasing human energy to productively utilize the available resources.

ACKNOWLEDGMENTS

My immense gratitude to:
My wife Lupita, for her encouragement, comments, technical help, book design, and amazing patience!

My children: Elisabeth, Suzanne and Michael: for their editing, early reads and feedback.

James Beswick, Dick Buckles, Rob Bignell, Rex Hudson, and Brian Rush: for their comments and recommendations.

Dwayne House, Dick Rechtien and Stan Whitcomb: for a lifetime of business experience and friendship.

Our cat, Alley, for not sitting on my keyboard, and limiting her demand for attention to five times a day!

Without 'you all' this work would not have been attempted, let alone completed!

CONTENTS

The Ultimate Guide to Avoiding Business Start-Up Failure

INTRODUCTION:
FAILURE IS THE NORM

"...there is nothing more difficult to carry out, nor more doubtful of success, nor more dangerous to handle, than to initiate a new order of things."
— Machiavelli, *The Prince*

A great feeling of relief and satisfaction surged through me, as I lay by the pool of a dingy downtown Miami apartment building. That afternoon I had reached a settlement with my remaining major creditor. Now, looking up at the moon and swatting at the mosquitoes, I thought about my financial situation. On balance I decided my net worth was precisely zero, and that was fine. In fact, it was better than fine because I had managed to work my way up to zero from a deficit of a million dollars.

What had brought me to this point was the financial collapse of my business. Not for the first time, and not for the last time, I optimistically regarded the future, ignored the 100% humidity, disregarded my lack of capital, and began planning my next business venture.

In total, thus far in my career, I have started thirty businesses. As a result I am now a grizzled, and somewhat battered, veteran with many stories to tell about the wolves and sharks that roam the U.S. economy. Twenty five of these start-ups failed. Sometimes I lost my money slowly and steadily, and sometimes the process was brutal and quick. I have experienced fraud, theft, recessions, incompetent professionals, bad planning, partnership failure, inadequate profit, and the loss of all my customers. To these I added my own business errors of every shape and description.

Like a battered pugilist, I learned to duck and weave. Almost accidentally, as the lessons of the small business world seeped into my subconscious, I began to make better decisions. The result was that my businesses gradually became profitable and the cash flows turned positive. From my successes I was able to build capital with which to make bigger investments and, in effect, to take bigger risks.

Contemplating my start-up experience, I came to the shocking and cathartic realization that my actions and endeavors had been seriously flawed. In hindsight, I am amazed at how long it took me to understand that my senior executive experience in Fortune 500 companies did not translate well into the small business field. At least, it did not for me.

In writing this book I examined the causes of my many failures and the process that led to the fewer number of successes. My conclusion is that twenty factors correlated most closely to my failures – and their converse correlated, in the main, with my successes.

To test the relevance of the factors numerically, I assigned each factor a score of 0 to 5. For example the factor "Inadequate Desire and Motivation" was assigned a score of 5 when I was not particularly motivated by a particular business. In those cases where I was really excited by a business I gave this factor a score of 0. In this way, I rated each of the factors for each of my start-ups. I then totaled the scores for each business.

The average score for my 25 failures was 77.5. For my 5 successful start-ups the average score was 30.2. These lower "failure scores" meant that the successful businesses, or rather "non-failures", had a lower correlation to the 20 failure factors than the start-ups which failed.

The factors and scores for each business were compiled into a Failure Scoring Model which is shown in the Appendix.

A high "failure score" for a start-up business may be compared to a high golf handicap. This comparison would be even closer if the average golf course had 20 holes instead of the standard 18.

Taking this example one step further consider an entrepreneur who scored many 5s on the twenty factors. For example there might be lack of working capital, poor marketing and inadequate accounting knowledge. This entrepreneur would tend to be cut after the first round (year one) of a championship competition. He would not get to play in the second round (year two) – let alone have a chance to remain in business for the long haul.

Three of my failures had very high scores. One was a Temporary Help business with a score of 96, another was Used Car Sales with a score of 95, and, the third was a Spring Water Distribution business also with a score of 95. Had I used the Failure Scoring Model before starting those ventures, the outcome might have been different – that is, if I had applied myself to improving my score, by lowering my handicap.

The average score for each factor is shown at the end of the pertinent chapters. At this point the reader may gain a clearer understanding of the scoring method by reviewing the model in the Appendix.

Since I was successful 5 times out of 30 tries my success rate was 17%. That is, I failed 83% of the times I came to the plate - to switch the analogy from golf to baseball!

This rate of failure is worse than that of the average entrepreneur – but not by a country mile. In 1989, Dunn and Bradstreet reported that 52% of firms failed during their first five years in business. More recently, in 2007, a U.S. Bureau of Labor Statistics study found that only 38% of the businesses opened in 1998 survived five years later – that is 62% failed in their first five years in business. This rate of failure has continued, if not accelerated, in the dire circumstances of the Great Recession and its aftermath.

Business failure - not business success, is the fate in store for the hopes and dreams of most entrepreneurs. That is the norm!

These percentages should raise the antennae of every entrepreneur, and of all concerned with small business and the growth of the economy. On a U.S.-wide basis, more than 50 percent of non-farm production is generated by small business. Perhaps of even greater importance, with unemployment so high at present, small business is the source of most new job creation. Thus even a small reduction in start-up failures would have a meaningful impact on employment and gross domestic product.

Entrepreneurs rarely consider that they could end up as a statistic - a failure. Their ego is more likely to cause them to believe "that will not happen to *me!*" Recognizing the possibility of failure should not stop the entrepreneur from starting a new business. The key is to find a point of balance between daring and caution, and, between realism and hope.

I strongly believe that budding entrepreneurs will improve their chances of survival and success by studying the failure factors and the model. They will further improve their chances if they rate their own start-ups against each factor. By doing their homework they will be on their way to learning the extremely complex and difficult trade of the entrepreneur.

SUMMARY

Start-up failure is the norm. A high percent of businesses do not make it past the first few years. The reduction of this failure rate offers an enormous opportunity to save time and resources. Based on my experience with 30 start-ups 20 factors correlate closely with failure. These factors are validated through a Failure Scoring Model which entrepreneurs may use to evaluate their own start-ups.

ACTION

Entrepreneurs - score your own start-up using the Failure Scoring Model. Then develop and act on a plan to lower your scores on each factor. This will improve your chances of success and reduce your chances of failure.

1

INADEQUATE DESIRE AND MOTIVATION

Many people dream of starting a business and becoming as successful as Bill Gates of Microsoft, Warren Buffet of Berkshire Hathaway or Jeff Bezos of Amazon. Others simply want to be their own boss – to be in business for themselves. Yet again others want to opt out of the savage game of corporate politics or just set their own hours. In a recession, layoffs increase, and people open businesses as an alternative to finding, or may be not finding, a new job.

However establishing and running you own business requires total dedication and commitment. Without this it would be better to adjust your sights to a more conventional career or perhaps to the adoption of a money-making hobby, or sideline business. Desire and motivation cannot be manufactured by telling yourself how much you want success. Nor is it enough to desire independence or money, or prestige or whatever else a successful business might bring you. In effect these constitute an attempt to bribe yourself into doing something that, at heart, you may not really want to do.

To put into a start-up business the kind of dedication necessary for success, the work *itself* must be something you love. The work must be your passion.

My own first attempt at being in business for myself – which was also my first failure – serves as an illustration.

Before that, let us consider what led me to this objective in the first place. It came partly from my father who was a successful upper level manager installing telephone exchanges during the day. At night and on weekends, he developed and installed automatic turnstiles to help maximize the crowd that could enter soccer stadiums. I learned little about this business from him, though I formed an opinion that part-time start-ups just buried you in extra work. I decided that if I ever had my own business, it would be full-time.

My main motivation came from hearing about my grandfather who owned a typical English green grocers shop that sold fruits and vegetables. To buy his produce, he travelled to Covent Garden wholesale market before dawn, every day, in all kinds of weather. He was very careful with his money and his family lived frugally in a few rooms above the shop. When he retired 35 years later, he invested his savings in stocks and shares. However he lost most of his money in an Argentinean market crash. With what was left of his savings he went back into business, and opened another green grocers shop. He turned this into another success in much less time with all his prior experience. This let him retire again and live comfortably in a suburb of London.

His story impressed me and one day, while at college, I told him I wanted to follow in his footsteps and have my own business one day. He grumped in reply, "Well, you've done nothing yet!" - For in his mind my college education was a waste of time. He had started work at thirteen, and I was still studying at the age of 21. This was a bit of an injury to my psyche and part of my motivation has always been to show him!

The successful career of British millionaire tycoon Sir Charles Clore (1904-1979) also motivated me. I decided to emulate him and become a millionaire myself. At the time in 1954, this was equivalent to $2.8 million U.S. By 2012 I would need $24 million inflation adjusted dollars to reach that goal, and I can assure you I have a long way to go! What is more it was not, in fact, a realistic measure of success to begin with.

From a practical point of view, my life-long goals – to be as successful and independent as my grandfather, and make a lot of money – were of no real value in helping me make a success at any given enterprise.

The major problem I had at the start was that I had no idea how to begin. I did not have a mentor and I had not read many books on small business start-ups. While playing with various business ideas, I worked for large corporations in England, and in the United States.

Among my early ideas were to import leather products from Morocco, sewing needles from India, and port wine cheese from England. Another business idea was to help home builders with a computerized estimating and project management system. However, these were just ideas that I pursued for only a few months.

Meanwhile, I continued my career as a part of different corporate machines. I was a salary man, a suit, a white shirt executive, a ladder climber. Eventually, I was promoted to Vice President and Controller at a NYSE company. My future was secure. I had an excellent salary, annual bonus, a staff of skilled employees and managers, a full-time highly qualified executive secretary, substantial life insurance, full family medical coverage, a pension plan, stock options, and a chrome bumper Mercury Marquis corporate car. Further there was potential for promotion, or to move on to a higher position in another corporation.

Despite this success, I still had the itch to be in business for myself. Finally I made up my mind to resign and become a stock market and commodities trader.

However, I did not have a business plan, and I did not have a realistic understanding of what was needed to succeed in that field. I had not read *Security Analysis* by Benjamin Graham (with David Dodd), nor *The Intelligent Investor*, which were so valuable to Warren Buffett.

Without a computer, living in Miami over a thousand miles away from Wall Street, and with no real investment experience, I took control of my stock account and started trading. The value of my portfolio went up and down, without significant net growth during my first year of full time day trading. Moreover – and more importantly – I discovered that I was not excited by the work. In fact, I was bored. When boredom and lack of motivation reached a peak, I returned to the corporate world as Vice President, Finance of a mid-size local company.

My first real attempt to work for myself had ended in failure. But it provided me with an important lesson in what causes a business to fail and conversely what can lead to success.

The seeds of business or investment success are found in the things you like to do in your spare time. These should be included in the business that you choose to start. Then you will not just be working, you will be engaged in a beloved hobby. Your work will not be drudgery, but something you would do, even if it paid you nothing at all. Time will fly by, and you will find yourself putting long hours into your business as naturally as play.

As a result of this dedication and deep interest, you will achieve competence and expertise in your chosen field. This is more satisfying than working at something that you are already competent at but don't enjoy doing very much! By going into a business in which you do something you enjoy, you can avoid burnout or regret over the long hours required to make the business successful.

SUMMARY

Becoming self-employed or starting your own business requires a very strong motivation. As events unfold, the strength of that desire will be tested by the problems that abound in a small business start-up, and the long hours required. Nearly always, a deep enjoyment and passion for the work, is required to press on to success.

ACTION

Entrepreneurs should ensure that they deeply enjoy and are passionate about the business they have selected to start. They should also read *"Awaken the Giant Within: How to Take Immediate Control of Your Mental, Emotional, Physical and Financial Destiny!"* by Anthony Robbins.

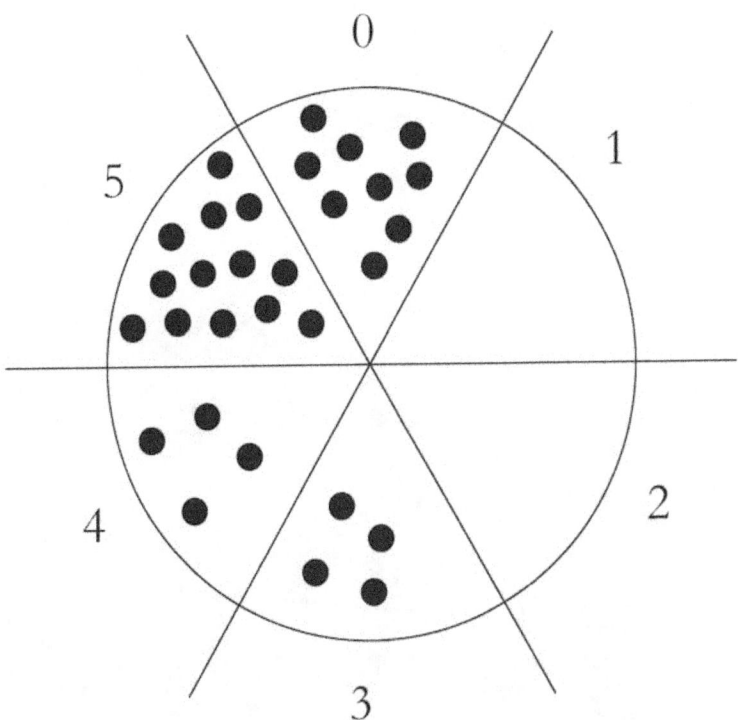

Desire & Motivation

SCORING

Average score of my failures: 3.7 – out of worst case 5.
(too often I did not really enjoy the work required)

Average score of my successes: 0
(best level – I was truly motivated)

Score this factor for yourself _____?

2

NEGATIVE CASH FLOW

Cash flow is a concept that many entrepreneurs do not fully grasp, yet it is an essential factor in business survival. Over time, negative cash flow will drive any business into the abyss.

Simply put, when all cash receipts exceed all cash payments in a day, or week or month then cash flow is considered to be positive for that period of time. On the other hand, when cash out exceeds cash in, then the cash flow is negative. In the words of Charles Dickens, "Annual income twenty pounds, annual expenditure nineteen pounds and sixpence, result—happiness. Annual income twenty pounds, annual expenditure twenty pounds and sixpence, result—misery."

In April 2012, on the TV show *Madmen*, the show's advertising agency ran short of money. They had needed to front the expense of development work for a new client.

Unfortunately, while the billings were strong, they had to wait for payment on the client's accounts payable process. In the interim, their staff had to be paid, rent, utilities, and other overhead expense incurred. Their cash flow was negative, and the partners did not take Christmas bonuses. This led their English finance manager, who desperately needed money, to commit fraud. Eventually this led to his suicide in a later episode.

Lucky the start-up that is funded by investors with deep pockets, or that has access to venture capital funding. Such start-ups may run cash negative for a long time and keep turning to their "rich uncles" so to speak. To some extent, FedEx and Amazon were businesses that grew to profitability after long periods of negative cash flow. Similarly, new gold mines or oil drilling operations require large cash investments to cover negative cash flow that may payoff big if they make a good find.

However the average start-up needs to reach positive cash flow as quickly as possible. It is rare that businesses do this right out of the starting gate. But they need to achieve positive cash flow before their limited supply of starting capital is exhausted. Once positive cash flow is achieved this must be continued, or new funds secured from the owner or from outside sources. Most entrepreneurs will need to become financing specialists using methods such as family loans, credit cards and vendor financing. A useful reference here is the book *Guerrilla Financing* by Bruce Blechman and Jay Conrad Levinson.

A common reason for failing to generate and maintain positive cash flow is by expanding too quickly or unwisely. My venture into apartment building ownership in the early 1980s failed for this reason. I started with the purchase of a

13-unit building in a deteriorating neighborhood with funds that I derived from a second mortgage on my home.

Without prior experience in the business, I learned how to prepare leases, collect the rent, give three days notices, assess late fees and work my way through the county eviction process. Utility bill deposits and address changes were tasks that I had delegated to accounts payable clerks when I worked in the corporate world. However, I now had to do them myself. I also learned to make small repairs, clear sinks and snake sewer lines. One toilet remained blocked no matter how much I plunged it. Finally I yanked the toilet and turned it upside down to find that the tenant had thrown a large meat bone down which had stuck in the S bend. Running into this type of problem was not my cup of tea but my active involvement helped ensure positive monthly cash flow from the start.

Wanting to grow as quickly as possible, I decided to acquire a 25 unit apartment building. The financing was arranged through the seller who accepted a wraparound mortgage. In addition, I set up a limited partnership that bought the 13 units and the new 25 unit building. This returned to me my original cash. In effect I owned a 50% interest in the overall investment, with none of my own money invested. This was my first application of the methods covered in Robert Allen's excellent book *Nothing Down: How to Buy Real Estate with Little or No Money Down.*

Unfortunately, I was more enamored with the deal making than with the operations. In addition, I did not pay attention to one of Bob Allen's other recommendations - "never buy in a poor area."

Within a few months I had an opportunity to buy a well located 50 unit apartment building. This had no deferred maintenance, full occupancy and positive cash flow. I kept this property for only two years, until I found a larger 70 unit building. I could not resist it and sold the 50 units to raise cash to make the down payment. Had I kept these buildings, the mortgages would have been paid off by now and I would be the owner of cash flow properties worth $10 million.

However this was not to be as my eyes were too big for my tummy, and I could not resist buying two *more* buildings in Hollywood, Florida. These ran at a negative cash flow as the mortgage financing was at 18%. Paul Volker at the Federal Reserve was fighting inflation, and mortgage interest tables started at 10% and rose as high as 20%.

The high interest rates and negative cash flow did not stop my acquisition program. Over a period of four months I acquired five more buildings containing 200 apartments in Miami Beach. For capital, I secured second mortgages on my existing properties and set up new limited partnerships. My new tenants were mostly low-income retirees and recent Mariel refugees. There was one happy note as one of the building managers was a 90-year-old lady. She had a splendid sense of humor and a forceful personality. We became friends, and occasionally on Sundays we would go out to breakfast, and, we would laugh and laugh.

The new properties had a lot of deferred maintenance. They needed new roofs, new carpets, paint and new air-conditioners in order to attract a better class of tenants. However I was short of funds for capital improvements, and the business was cash flow negative $15,000 per month. Moreover I realized that I had not included a management fee for myself in the budget, and I was scrambling to pay my own living expenses.

Within six months of acquiring the last of the Miami Beach properties, I was desperate to sell. I was a serious "don't wanter." My need to get rid of those properties was so intense that I accepted low ball offers and deals with extended payment terms. Two of the properties went into foreclosure. One I sold for a combination of opals, exchange trade units and a lesser amount of cash. On that deal, I ended up owing the buyer. He agreed to accept a note payable from me! The next day I decided to offer him some of the opals to clear the debt. When he took back some of the choicest stones I felt like a complete idiot. However I had dumped a really negative cash flow property, and I had some value in exchange for the property.

To rub salt into my wounds, South Beach real estate began a multi-year boom soon after I sold out. In hindsight, I could have taken advantage of this timing if I had been content to hold onto the positive cash flow properties while I learned more about the business. However, I did not, and I was out of the apartment business with a bloody nose. In memory of those days I have an award plaque from my real estate broker stating I had sold $4 million of real estate in the year – yes I did, but I lost my shirt in the process.

SUMMARY

Most start-ups run at a negative cash flow rate during the early months and years. Product development, market penetration and the development of a viable business model frequently require more loan or equity capital than expected. Failure to budget, run the business frugally and other missteps may extend this period beyond the entrepreneur's ability to find additional capital. My venture into apartment building ownership failed because of unexpected major repairs and excessive operating costs magnified by overexpansion. Negative cash flow was my comeuppance.

ACTION

The entrepreneur should learn all about cash flow before starting a business. Then it is essential to monitor operating cash flow weekly and monthly. If the potential entrepreneur feels completely at sea on this subject then a simple exercise is to prepare a household cash flow budget for several months before venturing into a real business start-up.

Cash Flow

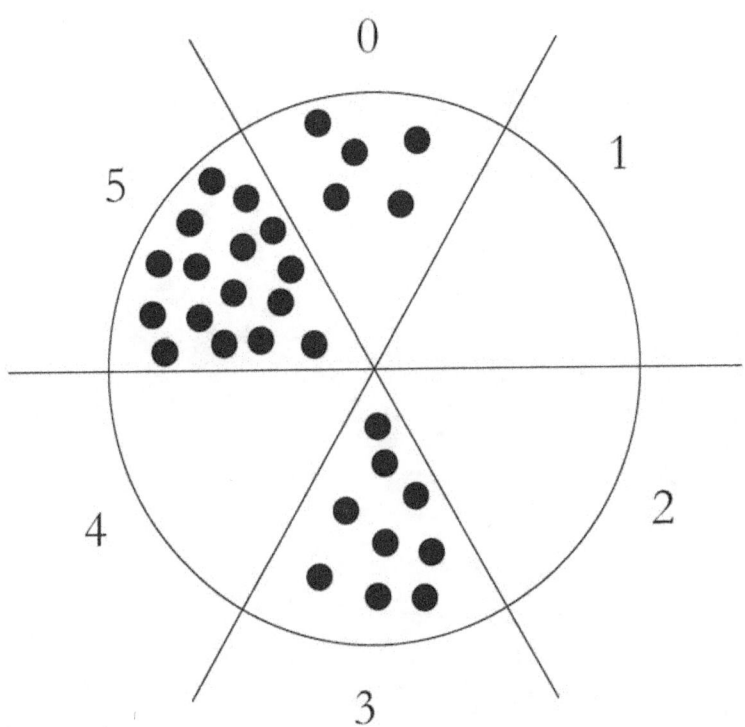

SCORING

Average score of my failures: 3.9
(out of worst case 5)
Average score of my successes: 1.8
(a good performance – I was watching my cash)

Your score is _____?

3

THE WRONG INDUSTRIES

Hordes of fortune seekers rushed to the Californian goldfields in 1849, and later to the Yukon in Canada. A few gold miners became rich but most remained poor or were forced to take up more mundane work. More people found success opening saloons, stores, banks and other services that catered to the prospectors. The same thing happened when diamonds were discovered in South Africa. One man, Cecil Rhodes, became so rich and powerful that he was able to go on to carve out the nation of Rhodesia. But men by the thousands spent their lives looking for the one strike that would make them rich, only to give up after a lot of wasted time and money.

The start-up entrepreneurs in high-tech industries such as the Internet and social media are today's miners. In their case, not only is the Mother Lode elusive, but when found, may change its "location" with little warning. Due to the rate of change, both the entrepreneur and his company must regularly reinvent themselves to survive and grow. The number of business failures in such fields is very high, even higher than the failure rate for small business start-ups in general.

In the early days of the Internet, I started a web-based parts distribution business. For a year, I worked on the development with a tech savvy partner until he grew tired of the endeavor and set up an entirely different business – an English Pub. Still intent on making the business work I funded a full time developer. However, when we went live the market response was underwhelming and costs were disproportionally high. My great hope of competing with Amazon fizzled.

Another of my web selling ideas was a joint project with the manufacturer of inkjet products. My end included the development of the web site, but lack of a marketing focus and partner disagreements led me to close this business also.

A glutton for punishment I invested in yet another web based start-up. This was to be a stock photography vendor. This business was no more successful. Over a year was spent developing the website and acquiring and creating the photos. By the time we were ready to launch, technology had overtaken us, and the price of stock photographs had fallen precipitously. Cell phones and digital cameras had become ubiquitous and the market was glutted. It was necessary to fold up shop, and fold up is what we did.

The problem isn't the Internet *per se*. It's a pair of common problems with fields that are new and hot. First, they attract a horde of would-be entrepreneurs all competing for a limited market. Secondly, they evolve so rapidly, being industries in embryo as it were, that staying on top of things is almost impossible. Going for the "Latest Big Thing" entrepreneurs tend to be dazzled by unrealistic visions of unlimited success. This, together with a lack of understanding of the work required, is another reason for start-up failure.

The entrepreneur will find a more likely path to success in older, better established, but still growing industries. Warren Buffett, a mega billionaire, has proven the effectiveness of this strategy by investing in businesses as mundane as insurance, food and house wares.

Other fields to consider include education and health. Start-ups in those fields have a 44% survival rate after seven years while information businesses have a 24% survival rate over the same period. This was reported in an article by Knaup and Piazza, *Business Employment Dynamics data: Survival and Longevity,* in Monthly Labor Review, U.S. Bureau of Labor Statistics.

Another useful source of comparative industry survival rates was provided by Scott Shane in a 2010 contribution to the online service *"Small Business Trends."* He found that 57.4% of finance, insurance and real estate start-ups in 2000 survived five years later. On the other hand, the survival of start-ups in transportation, communication and utilities was only 44.4%. Scott pointed out that while the current economic climate would probably impact negatively on the first category the chances of creating a long lived business are greater in some industries than others.

An added advantage of entering an established industry is that higher quality and more accurate business plans may be prepared with the help of industry consultants, advisors, seminars and trade groups.

SUMMARY

Industry selection is a critical step for the entrepreneur. Those who select new industries, new technologies and new products are exposed to a high risk of failure. They are akin to gold miners and gamblers. To reduce the risk of failure entrepreneurs should concentrate on basic services and products in an established but growing industry.

ACTION

Spend time considering the field or industry in which you will spend much of your working life. Will the demand for your product still be there when you are ready to deliver? And how long will that demand remain?

Industry Selection

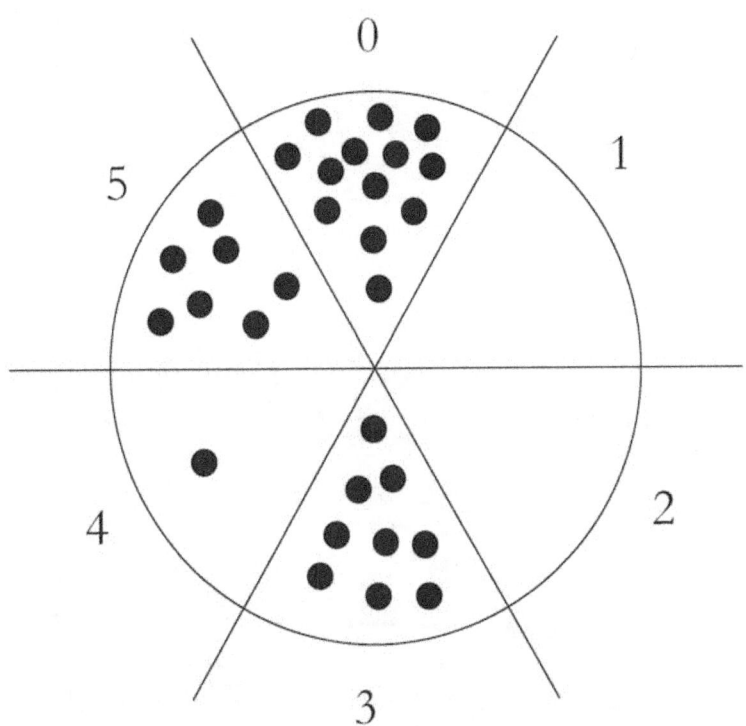

SCORING

Average score of my failures: 2.5
(out of worst case 5)

Average score of my successes: 0.6
(an important factor in my successes)

Your score is _____?

4

DID NOT SERVE AN APPRENTICESHIP IN THE INDUSTRY

There are many fields where participants must acquire specific training, serve an apprenticeship, pass examinations, become licensed and fulfill continuing education requirements. Examples include lawyers, nurses, insurance agents, real estate brokers, appraisers, electricians and general contractors. This type of training and apprenticeship brings the entrepreneur to the starting gate. Only then does the entrepreneur begin to acquire experience in the field and in running a business.

Even if the field selected for a start-up does not have licensing requirements the entrepreneur should consider gaining the necessary knowledge, skills and experience in advance. This is a *practical* requirement – apprenticeship is an essential factor in success!

My foray into general contracting was more by accident than design. Certainly I did not serve an apprenticeship or take a test. What happened was that a licensed general contractor approached me for financing help on a school refurbishment project. He needed working capital to pay for his workers and supplies. Payments on such projects are usually due only after each phase is complete and verified. I agreed to act as funder and financial controller for 50 percent of the profits. In my mind, this was a low-risk, minimum involvement financing investment. And so it turned out to be as the work was completed on time, we were paid per the agreement and I earned a fair return on my investment.

The contractor then won a larger sub-contract to renovate a student housing project. Again I provided the working capital and acted as financial controller, while his job was to handle the contracting work. However, it turned out he did not have the skills needed to administer a project of this size. To help out, I found myself involved in operations, hiring workers for demolition, sheet rock, drywall, electric, plumbing and painting – areas in which I had no experience. I needed help myself so I hired a foreman. He in turn knew a painter with a team of four men. On an inspection tour, I grew concerned when I saw the painters sanding without masks, gloves or construction helmets. Things got worse when the painter was deported and his wife demanded prepayment before she would let the men finish the job. I went further out of pocket to keep the job progressing.

Compounding the problems I realized that my contractor partner was misreading the drawings, and even was deriving incorrect quantities and materials specifications. Both he and the subs missed the need for fire resistant drywall. In desperation I studied the technical drawings and questioned everyone as to what they needed bought and delivered to the site.

Another shock was that the foreman was underestimating the labor hours needed. He was a good individual craftsman but not an effective manager. To avoid overruns I was forced to prepare the work schedules and manpower assignments for him as well.

Contract administration and billing was an area in which I had no knowledge. Luckily my son had some experience and he advised me how to file lien notices. The timely filing of 'notices to owner' saved the day when the main contractor was fired for non-performance. We were paid for our work on Phase I because the owner made release of our lien a requirement before the contractor was paid. After that, the job was shut down, and the money we had pre-spent on Phase 2 supplies was down the drain. It was touch and go, but since our liens were perfected we came out even. I wanted no more to do with this risky business and so we closed down. This start-up should never have got off the ground. I did not know the industry and I did not understand the skill set that my partner brought to the table. Not having served an apprenticeship I was too green for words.

SUMMARY

Casual entry into industries of which you have little knowledge is almost certain to lead to failure. Businesses like contracting are best left to the trained, experienced entrepreneur with an excellent team, a business plan and substantial financing.

ACTION

Entrepreneur, make sure you serve an apprenticeship in the industry you chose and learn it from the ground up to the executive level - before starting your own venture.

Apprenticeship

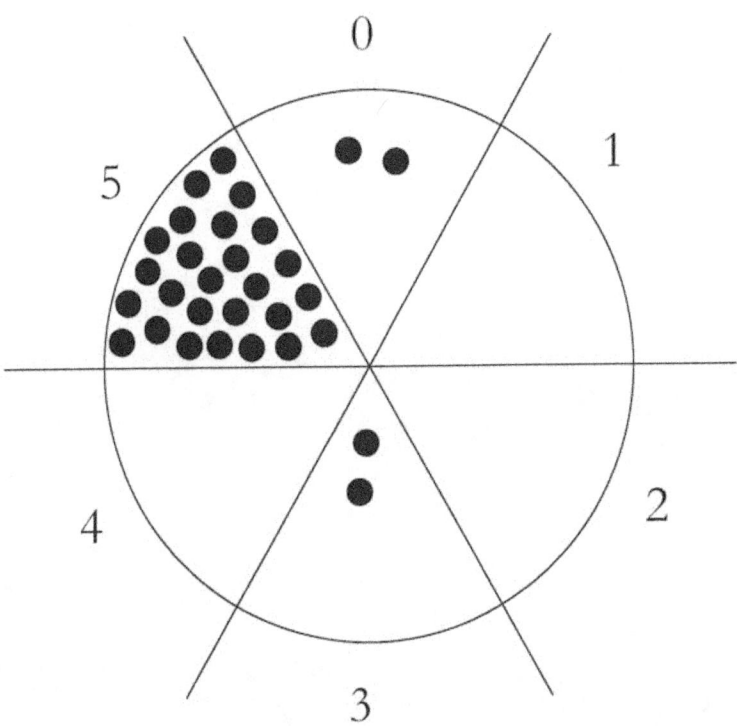

SCORING

Average score of my failures: 4.9
(virtually no time spent in apprenticeship
almost guaranteed failure)

Average score of my successes: 2.6
(even here I did not obtain enough
advance experience)

Your score is _____?

5

THE WRONG PARTNERS

In the first five years of my entrepreneurial career, I operated alone. I consulted no one. I set up the entities, found investors or provided the capital myself. I then managed and operated the businesses. This gave me independence and complete control, but it eventually led to financial collapse and the loss of my house.

One of the problems was that when a business settles into the day to day nitty-gritty of operations, I lose interest. What I needed, but did not have, was an operations-oriented partner to keep the business on track once it was up and running. My great interest is in the start-up process, and, in business problem solving, financing and, planning and analysis. After reaching this conclusion, I began to actively seek business associates with whom to partner. But that, too, led to new problems as it turned out – surprise, surprise –

that my partners had interests and personalities of their own. What I needed was a set of partner selection criteria.

One of the most important is that each partner should have a similar financial motivation and loyalty to the partnership. I came to this conclusion after a really disastrous investment went south. What happened was that I bought into a dealership taking up 49% of the shares. Unknown to me the "owner" of the 51% had an undisclosed arrangement with his prior partners. I continued happily along thinking we were of one mind and jointly running the business. The second problem was that my due diligence had failed to reveal that the business was on the brink of financial collapse. When the majority owners filed for bankruptcy our entire investment was lost.

How did I feel, you might ask? Shocked and amazed at my naivety certainly, but mostly bewildered as to how it had happened. As I studied the event I concluded that the most positive way to view this experience was to think "thanks for the lesson" and move on. In addition I promised myself to conduct in depth due diligence in future, and to secure at least a 50% ownership interest in any new partnership.

Another partnership failed when I realized that my partner was not applying his energy equally to mine. I felt resentful and that was not constructive for a good working relationship. From this experience I learned to define duties in advance and to base pay and distributions on the work done as well as the ownership percentage. Thus if one partner is 100% committed to operations and the other is less involved, then the first should receive a greater reward prior to any partner distributions.

However this may lead to a difference in motivation between operating partners and non-operating partners with respect to pay and benefits. Operating partners may prefer to maximize personal earnings rather than partnership distributions particularly when they hold a minority interest.

This can and does result in "country club management" which indulges itself in perks, bonuses, pensions, cars, excessive expense reports, unnecessary memberships, sports tickets, first-class travel, expensive furnishings, large offices and landscaped grounds. If there is a large enough operating cash flow then the "country club management" will arrange/push for the business to buy planes and boats of ever increasing size and luxury. These "partners" spend partnership money on their own lifestyles rather than on the distribution of dividends to their co-investors.

Having known your prospective partner in school or in a prior business is very beneficial. However you still need to objectively evaluate their skills and abilities, and to clearly define each partner's organizational role. Business partnerships are like marriages: Compatibility is essential. If one partner is dominant and strongly assertive, then the other must be willing to take a supportive role. Otherwise there will be nothing but conflict and argument. We have all seen the adverts, "For Sale – partners cannot agree."

One area of potential disagreement is when the partner capital accounts are out of balance. The difference should be compensated at a flat percentage rate per year before equity distributions. I use and recommend that the rate be set at 10%. This provides motivation for partners with surplus capital to lend to the partnership. In addition third-party lenders may classify partner loans as subordinated debt. This may help improve the calculation of the debt to equity ratio.

The employment of family members is a particularly sensitive topic. Their employment and pay should be subject to approval by all partners. This avoids accusations of nepotism down the road. On several occasions I have noticed that family and friends are hired and rewarded in excess of their contribution. This is a source of contention and possibly secret resentment that may damage the viability of the partnership and the business.

Another source of potential partner disagreement is unequal non-business expenses and draws. To correct this, the partners should agree on a procedure to adjust these in the capital accounts. This includes disproportional travel, purchases and unusual expenses such as sports events or subscriptions.

Perhaps the most important recommendation is to ensure that the original partnership agreement addresses a way to end the relationship if it runs onto the rocks. This is essential when the partners have equal 50:50 participation - the balance that I prefer. In my view, it is critical to have pre-thought out procedures to resolve situations where "partners cannot agree."

SUMMARY

Many entrepreneurs join with partners without enough thought. To reduce risk of business and partnership failure it is essential to go through a rigorous selection process and determination of compatibility. Partner loans should be well compensated. A balanced ownership of 50:50 is preferred. The original agreement must provide for a method for separation, should that become necessary.

ACTION

Entrepreneur, find capable, agreeable partners to balance your short comings, and use a lawyer to carefully prepare the partnership agreement that details the method of separation.

The Wrong Partners

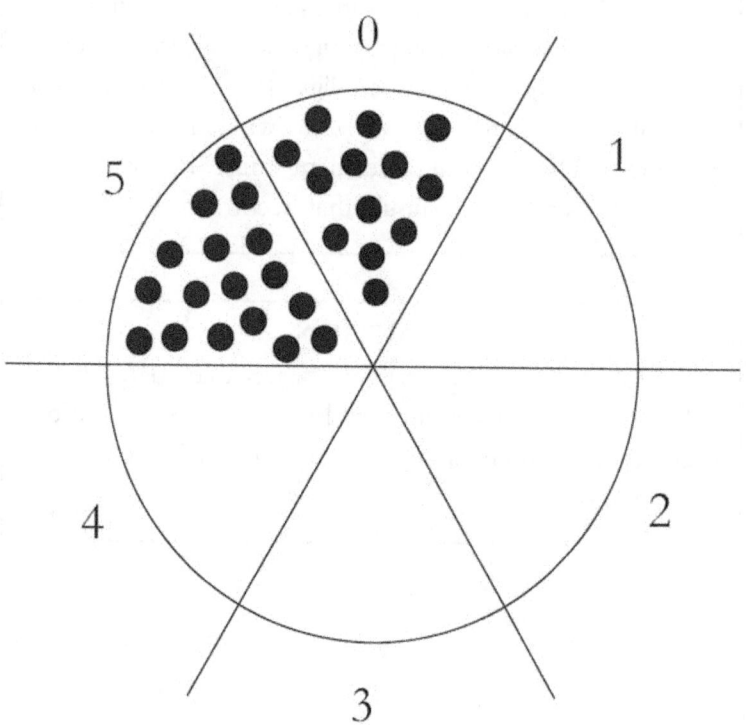

SCORING

Average score of my failures: 3.4
(bad situations led to necessary learning)

Average score of my successes: 0
(excellent partners and good agreements)

Your score is _____?

6

LACK OF SMALL BUSINESS EXECUTIVE EXPERIENCE

Make no mistake about it: running a small business requires a skill set that must be acquired through experience. If you have been a top level manager of a small business you have probably acquired some of these skills and are ahead of the game. But if you have never run a business before, you will have to learn on the job. That means you will have to learn from your mistakes – and those mistakes may be serious enough to cause your new venture to fail.

What is more, each industry has its own skill set requirement. There are always nuances and unspoken methods that the old hands know and the new guy does not. While there is a certain amount of overlap, if your experience was in a completely different industry, then you can be certain you will have learning to do with the attendant risk of error.

In a pattern that I have repeated throughout my career, I learned these truths the hard way. One example was when I became CEO of a temporary help agency. A friend of mine told me he wanted to retire and offered me a half interest with payments to him over time. I was to have full control and he would be a silent investor. It was a nothing down deal, and I can never resist those. Of course, if my English forefathers were around they would have told me to look the "Gift Horse in the Mouth." That analogy references the old method of inspecting a horse's teeth to see how old it is. The actual expression is "Don't Look a Gift Horse in the Mouth."

For several months revenues were strong. We sent out crews to help clean up after a hurricane, crews to do the dirty work at a recycling plant and a special female crew to work at a clothing manufacturer. However gradually the hurricane labor requirement declined and the conditions at the recycling plant made it difficult to find full crews. To replace this lost revenue, I pushed our sales staff and found it necessary to go out on calls myself.

The most serious problem was worker compensation insurance. This came to light when an auditor from the insurance company identified that employees had been assigned to lower than appropriate risk categories. This had reduced premium expense in prior years but now I was faced with a $100,000 catch up bill including penalty and interest. Lacking industry knowledge I had not challenged the pre-accepted method used by the accounting function. In addition our accident experience and cost was excessive as we did not have an effective accident prevention program, nor did we closely monitor injured workers so that they came back to work when able. We had been consistently underpaying our insurance policy, underestimating overall cost of labor, and failing to quote at realistic prices.

To make the business profitable required an investment in working capital to cover the worker comp shortfall and time to secure higher margin accounts. I had no available capital and my partner declined to invest more money. So there and then the die was cast. We agreed to close down the business and I folded up shop. Only six months elapsed from my initial enthusiastic buy-in until I turned the key in the lock for the final time. *"C'est la vie. C'est la vie!"* thought I, and off I went to my next adventure – may be a little wiser

If I had had any executive experience in the temporary help industry, I could have headed off many of these problems or seen how to solve them. My overall lack of experience in the field caused me to make mistakes that a more experienced executive would not have made.

SUMMARY

Prior industry experience is valuable, but prior top executive experience in the same industry is even better. If the entrepreneur lacks such experience, the risk of failure is very high - unless offset by industry knowledgeable co-workers, executives and partners.

ACTION

Do not go any further with your start-up until you have acquired executive level experience or help in that type of business.

Small Business Executive Experience

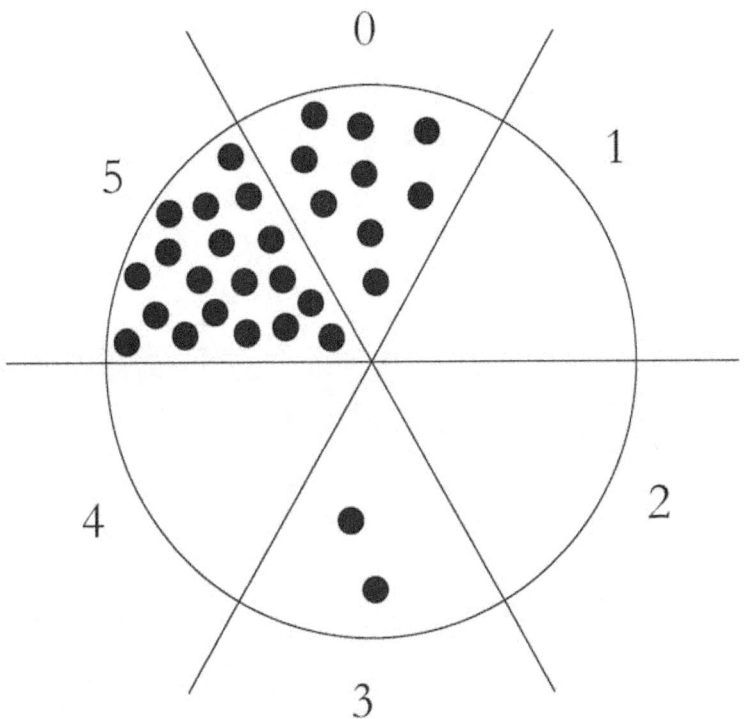

SCORING

Average score of my failures: 3.8
(I was crazy to not acquire prior executive experience)

Average score of my successes: 1.0
(it really helped to have that executive experience)

Your score is _____?

7

PHYSICAL, MENTAL OR
EMOTIONAL WEAKNESS

Tenacity, bootstraps and the willingness to work hard –
these are essential to entrepreneurial success. Working on
national holidays, midnight calls, up before the dawn, home
late at night and weekend meetings, are not unknown to small
business owners. They will rarely take vacations, and when
they do they will tend to take their work with them.

This is particularly true in the initial months and years.
Entrepreneurs who beat the odds and are successful with less
effort are few and far between.

Over time, long hours and hard work can take a heavy toll
on health and enjoyment of life. This is particularly true when
compounded with poor health habits such as smoking,
excessive drinking, poor diet and lack of exercise. For all of
these reasons, physical, mental or emotional weakness is
another common cause of business failure.

After my big financial comeuppance in my early days as an entrepreneur I found myself homeless though not quite penniless. My major debts were not yet resolved, but I still owned a car, a few clothes and some sticks of furniture. I was lucky that my children were at college or with their mother.

To settle some of my bills I sold my house and held a garage sale of my remaining valuable possessions. One of my greatest regrets was the sale of a wonderful painting by Popo and Ruby Lee. The subject was a semi-nude Native Indian girl and it had embarrassed my children for years, but I loved it. When my finances improved several years later I bought another in the same series from a Californian collector, and I have it still. However, the original had to go to pay college bills, and so it went.

Of enormous help was that my ex-partner had an unused office building at his engine distribution business. It comprised a small room, a toilet and a sink. The sink had one operating tap that provided only cold water. He let me use this office for a couple of months, and I set up a bed and a desk. After I installed a phone I carried on both my business and personal life from there.

In answer to worried inquiries from family and friends I would say, "I feel great," and I did. Every time I said "I feel great" a thrill went down my back. That simple positive exclamation still perks me up today. These words are the best tonic against negative thoughts that I know of.

Life was not entirely rosy in my new lodgings as I had a persistent ant problem. A local colony sent explorers into my room where they found my freshly-laundered shirts. For several days there was a line of ants from the front door to the clothes rack, up the rack, out onto the hangers, and down into their new rich mine of fresh starch. They were happy as clams, but I was a little perturbed, especially the first time I put on a shirt and the miners started to bite me. After jumping up and down and tearing off my shirt I decided that further action was needed. I had to protect my territory. For several minutes I stomped on ants, shook out shirts and progressed to the door where I attacked the remaining ant workers. Thus did I win the battle and regain sole possession of my new home and property.

However the ants were not finished. That night when I got into bed I found to my shock a great number of them, feeding off goodness knows what on my pillow! "That's enough!" I shouted and began a major ant eradication campaign. This led to a truce – thereafter they stayed outside the building, and I stayed inside.

My sojourn in the small office building came to an end when the facilities manager found out that I was living as well as running a financial consulting business from there. He complained that he needed the office for overflow staff and I had to move. Luckily, I was already hard at work on a new assignment, so I was earning enough to afford an apartment in a slightly less rough part of town.

While my living conditions in that single room with no hot water and starch-hungry ants may be somewhat beyond the norm, others have triumphed over much more difficult circumstances. What helped in my case was that I developed some very good habits regarding diet, exercise, and positive mind-set. I also made sure I went to bed before midnight and got a good night's rest. As I had quit smoking years before this was not a problem. In addition I still had a gym membership from my days as a corporate executive so I would shower and shave there after exercising. Without these, my health could easily have broken down.

There was a pool at my new apartment building and I began swimming laps. Later that summer I watched my son compete in a triathlon and I decided I could do that. So I added running and cycling to my aerobic workouts. Within two months I completed my first triathlon – an inappropriately named Sprint, with a 440 yards swim, 12 mile bike and 5K run to finish. I have continued to compete in triathlons for the last 25 years. The longest one was a one half ironman. This consisted of a 1.2 mile swim, followed by a 56 mile bike and a 13 mile run. While I did a good job and finished the race I felt really beat so I have kept to shorter distances ever since. My program of regular exercise has helped me maintain good health; and, a high energy level that has allowed me to keep working long after most people have retired.

As important as work ethic and physical health – perhaps more so – is positive thinking. Auto-suggestion is not superstition: Auto-suggestion works. I strongly believe that my subconscious mind works to implement my conscious thoughts, whether negative or positive. At bedtime, when I positively and firmly tell myself that I will find a solution to a problem or opportunity, then I awake frequently with the solution or a new approach. The same goes with the pre-sleep affirmation that I will attain my goals and objectives. In the morning I am up and at 'em with a positive attitude and making progress on those goals and objectives. This method of positive self-talk was brilliantly outlined in *The Amazing Results of Positive Thinking* by Norman Vincent Peale.

Positive thinking means never accepting, saying or thinking anything destructively negative about your own self. This does not mean that it's not important to evaluate errors and omissions that interfere with success and growth. But this evaluation needs to be objective and constructive, without putting yourself down: always with a view to making things better, not by condemning yourself.

Optimism has been an important ingredient in my life. When I emigrated from England to the United States it was with optimism for the future. Optimism led me to ask for my first car loan even though I had no credit. When my request was turned down I found a solution by buying a regular old flat iron from Montgomery Wards. They gave me immediate store credit. After I paid that bill, the bank loan officer accepted that I had established credit and made the loan!

Optimism has been a factor in every one of my start-ups. Optimism is required to walk up to potential customers and ask for their business. Optimism leads to exploration and the creation of new businesses without which economic advance would not occur.

Worry control is important in maintaining good mental health. At one time I used a day planner that came in a large three ring binder. These were sold by a realtor as a sideline business out of the trunk of his car. On one occasion he explained his method of controlling worry. This was to:

1. Write down specifically what is worrying you.
2. Think of the worst that could happen if the worry came true.
3. Accept the worst that could happen.
4. Build a plan to reduce or eliminate the worst that could happen.
5. Act positively on your plan.
6. Remain cheerful and optimistic with full belief in the certainty of your success.

SUMMARY

Newby entrepreneurs rarely comprehend how much work is required. The successful startup demands full dedication and time away from family and outside interests. The effort may place heavy physical and emotional demands on the body. Tenacity, self-belief and self-confidence are required to overcome adverse circumstances. These dangers and pitfalls can be overcome with the right knowledge and, even more importantly, with the right attitude and degree of optimism.

ACTION

Sit down and conduct a careful self-examination. Do you have the discipline and tenacity to travel the strenuous road to a successful start-up?

Physical, Mental & Emotional Strength

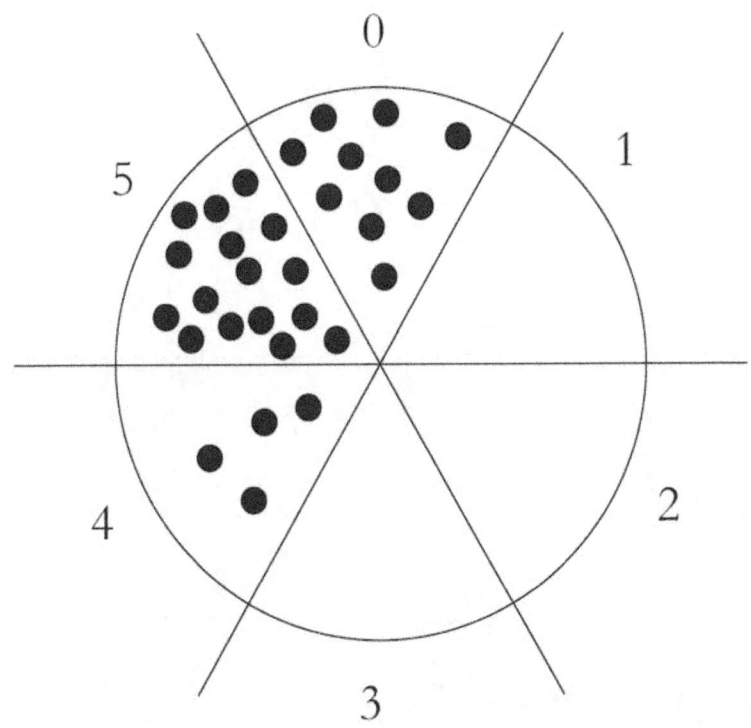

SCORING

Average score of my failures: 3.6
(tenacity was often the missing ingredient)

Average score of my successes: 0.6
(drive, energy, health and optimism galore)

Your score is _____?

8

BAD LEGAL AND ACCOUNTING ADVICE

In the key areas of accounting and law, quality advice is essential for start-up success. Unfortunately, incompetence is as likely to be found among these professionals, as in any other areas of life.

The specific legal structure and accounting method to adopt are among the most important decisions entrepreneurs make. Errors made in these areas may become more and more significant as the business grows. Therefore entrepreneurs should spend time understanding the options and effects of different approaches. In the decision process they should also consider the effect of potential growth and consider possible exit strategies – from the very beginning. If they have developed a well thought out business plan then this will provide a helpful reference for professional advisors.

For many years, I operated through limited partnerships. This business format limits the liability of the non-active partners (limited partners) to their original investment. The General Partner – my role - is responsible for actively operating the business and for guaranteeing and paying all debts of the business.

To reduce my personal liability, I took legal advice to form a corporation to take over the role of General Partner. I was President and CEO of the corporation and therefore had operating control. Corporations, provided they are operated legally, limit the liability of their shareholders to the amount invested.

However, when one of my limited partnerships ran into financial difficulty I did not use the limited liability afforded by the corporation. To partially compensate my limited partners I assigned to them the interest owned by my corporation. I knew this at the time – I was being too much the Boy Scout. I should have been more tough-minded. The limited partners had fully understood the deal, had their experts conduct full due diligence, and were qualified investors who accepted the risk going in.

In dealing with banks and mortgage lenders, I frequently signed guarantee forms that included specified joint and several liability clauses. My lawyers never explained the significance of this or perhaps I simply disregarded the risk. When a venture in which I had joint liability collapsed my bank account was drained by the lender. It was the most accessible asset. I finally understood that the lender will go after the easiest target and the deepest pockets. I have been on both sides of that sword. One time I had to settle up for all the partners, and in another case my financial partner had to pay off my debt obligation as well as his own.

From this experience I have come to two conclusions. The first is that guarantees are the same as loans and must be added to your own tolerance for total debt. The second is that lawyers' advice, if given, must be listened to carefully, evaluated, verified and respected.

Lacking proper legal and accounting advice, I have made the mistake of holding real estate in my own name, which has exposed all my assets to lawsuits. Suffice to say that an LLC is a better way to hold real estate since personal liability is reduced and there are other corporate, tax and organizational advantages.

For one start-up I was appointed President and CEO of a new corporation. This company secured financing for an investment in a new car dealership. Our corporate lawyer fell ill and was not available for the closing. My choice to replace him was a friendly lawyer who worked in an office near mine. He liked to wear light tan summer suits and a Panama hat. I guess I thought he would be savvy like the Southern lawyers in the movies. Predictably enough, this proved to be a poor basis for choosing a lawyer.

When the business went bankrupt, soon after we had completed our buy-in, I found that my country lawyer had failed to protect our interest. Far too late I realized that he had no experience with a corporate investment of this size and complexity. He was simply not competent for the task at hand, and in fact neither was I.

These experiences and others have ingrained in me the need to have the best possible representation, and to be completely practical and realistic about selecting a lawyer. In particular, it is a mistake to turn to a friend, or a prior business associate, unless you have direct knowledge of their capability in the specific area. Imprinted on my brain is the rule: never cut corners on cost when choosing critically important professional advisors.

Both large and small law firms and single practitioners should be considered. Larger practices will have backups available if your lawyer is unavailable or quits. They usually have a range of specialists on staff or in affiliation. Their disadvantage will be higher fees. For a small business they may assign an inexperienced junior, or poor performing senior. Look around the office and see how plush it is. Guess who pays for that? One alternative is to select a qualified small practice attorney. However that individual may be inundated by other work, be ill, go on vacation, or simply be unavailable when needed.

The selection process requires that the entrepreneur conduct interviews, establish compatibility, and ensure that the professional can explain issues in an understandable way. A specific recommendation on corporate formation should be discussed with each candidate. In this way the advantages and disadvantages will become clearer and candidate competence tested. As in any other key hiring decision, the entrepreneur should check references and talk with fellow businessmen who have used the attorney and the firm.

Ours is a country based on laws and our government likes to pass them. Because of this and the propensity to sue it is essential to stay current by regular meetings and phone calls with your legal representative. All companies must pay particular attention to pay, hours, health, pension, and disability laws. These are constantly changing and penalties can be very high for non-compliance.

Even when you have a competent attorney it is still essential to read every line of every document you sign. Lawyers do make mistakes but it is the client who ends up paying for them. Recently a very, very good lawyer, who I had used multiple times before, told me she could insert an existing signature page in a sale of shares document. But in the one case I was signing as trustee, and in the other I was signing as a corporate officer. These signature pages could not be substituted for each other. When I pointed this out, she immediately agreed, and the proper signature page was used. However it could have been that the entire conveyance was improper if I had not taken notice.

The selection of accounting and tax advisors also requires great care. The accountant should explain fees for services and be ready to help with all reporting needed for operations, lenders, investors, taxes, and payroll. There are just too many of these for the start-up entrepreneur to grasp without extended study and experience.

Entrepreneurs should use Certified Public Accountants (CPA) as accounting errors can endanger the survival of the business. In my experience it is important to check the work of accountants, as with lawyers, especially when tax returns are prepared. Even expert tax accountants will make mistakes while transcribing company financials to the IRS format. By checking the accountant's work the entrepreneur may learn ways to legally reduce taxes that the CPA may not have explained. Or perhaps the entrepreneur will finally grasp the importance of comments and recommendations that the CPA has been making for some time!

In all cases, it's important to remember that professional advice is just that - advice. It's not the lawyer or accountant who is liable for a mistake (except in cases of gross malfeasance). It is the client—which means it's you.

SUMMARY

Many CPAs and lawyers are not fully competent and make mistakes that can hurt the profitability if not the survival of the start-up. Entrepreneurs must take responsibility for all legal and accounting decisions regardless of the advice received. To do this, acquiring a proficient understanding of legal, accounting and tax reporting is necessary. Lawyers and CPAs must be selected as if the very survival of the business is at risk - because it is! All documents must be read - line by line - with the presumption that a mistake has been made, intentionally or not.

ACTION

The entrepreneur must ensure to hire competent legal and accounting professionals. Further, it is essential to fully understand and check their work.

Legal & Accounting Advice

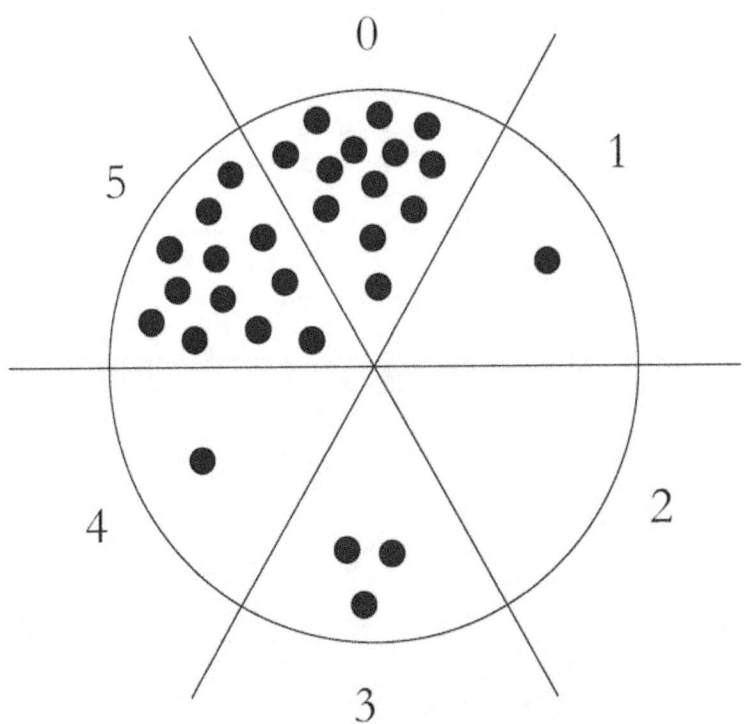

SCORING

Average score of my failures: 2.8
(very poor if not downright wrong in many cases)

Average score of my successes: 1.0
(not bad)

Your score is _____?

9

SHORTAGE OF WORKING CAPITAL

Working capital is the life blood of every business. It is a precious commodity, and securing it can be extremely difficult as well as time consuming. In the initial stage most entrepreneurs fund their businesses from savings, life insurance, credit cards, severance pay, vendor financing and personal loans from family and friends.

Bank loans are hard to secure for a start-up in the best of economic times, although some financing may be available through the SBA. At the time of writing in 2012 the banking system is recovering from its massive over-indulgence in sub-prime mortgages and the impact of the Great Recession. Underwriting standards are very tight, and small company loans and second mortgages are almost impossible to obtain without excellent credit, proof of a steady income and a significant down payment. In effect they have a sign up: 'No

Self-employed or Newby Entrepreneurs Need Apply.' Entrepreneurs should not waste much time seeking bank financing.

After being in business for two or three profitable years the entrepreneur may find bank officers willing to listen to their story. However smart entrepreneurs will develop a rapport with bank officers before this, so they come to know you and your business. In addition you will learn the bank's lending requirements early on. That way your business and reports may be structured to facilitate a favorable loan decision when this is possible.

Words of caution - banks are fair weather friends. They are not there to prop up developing and unprofitable enterprises. When the economy goes into a recession, banks may need to reduce their loan portfolios to enhance their own equity positions. To do this they may refuse additional funds, or demand pay down of commercial loans even from profitable businesses.

One method of securing working capital is to sell shares in the start-up. Perhaps an entrepreneur offers family and friends a 10 per cent participation for an investment of $10,000. From the investor's viewpoint this is only fair, as money is at risk on an untried idea, and possibly an untried entrepreneur. From the entrepreneur's viewpoint the same amount of capital ($10,000) may require only an offer of 5% participation once the business has been launched and has increased in value.

If venture capital providers become involved the entrepreneur's ownership may be diluted substantially, especially if additional rounds of financing are required. Thus to fund working capital entrepreneurs may find that borrowing money, even at high interest rates, is a viable alternative to giving up equity participation in the early start-up years.

Entrepreneurs frequently run out of working capital in building their businesses. Two completely different causes need attention. The first is that the entrepreneur's plans and expectations are frequently over-optimistic. At start-up sales are often slower and costs much higher than expected. Since break-even is delayed more working capital is required.

The second cause arises when the start-up becomes successful and the business really takes off. Entrepreneurs often think that profits will supply the extra working capital they need, but this is rarely the case. Think of it this way: If sales are $10,000 and net profit is 10% or $1,000, then cost of sales was $9,000. Now, if the entrepreneur must pay out the $9,000 before the $10,000 is collected then this is the amount of working capital required to support one month of sales. Since net profit was only $1,000 it will take 9 months to build enough working capital from profit – provided that every penny is retained in the business!

This problem is compounded when a successful sales program increases sales to $20,000 per month, an increase of 100%. Unfortunately the working capital requirement also increases by 100% to $18,000. In the real world, entrepreneurs run into this type of cash flow problem far too often and then frequently fail from lack of funds.

It may be helpful to read or reread the Cash Flow Chapter at this point!

Even investors with deep pockets run out of funds. As a rule of thumb, entrepreneurs should double their guestimate of the amount of working capital required to reach cash break-even. No matter how much planning has been done, I have found, time and time again, that this is the only way to be in the ballpark of the cash that will be needed.

With working capital usually very tight in the early days of a start-up, take home pay must be kept to a minimum. This is hard to do in the face of the public image of the high-flying entrepreneur. Confronted with news stories about start-ups which have gained venture capital interest it is easy to be dazzled by the mirage of quick returns.

However, most entrepreneurs should live on a shoestring while getting their companies off the ground. No money should be spent on unessential benefits, travel, meals, planes, boats and non-company cars. There should be no tickets to professional teams, no home phones, no boosted expense reports, and no non-working family on the payroll.

Every expense should be scrutinized and every penny squeezed. This practice should continue even when the business is profitable. Three quotations for each type of service and purchase should be a requirement. Discounts should be requested on a regular basis. Price reductions should be requested on every invoice including payments made to professionals.

To ensure staff is cost-conscious there should be regular meetings and memos on expenses as small as the number of paper clips, the use of scrap paper, and the reuse of file folders. In general, one should go for utility - not style.

Of course one can be "penny wise and pound foolish." Cost control must be balanced against the time required. In addition, advertising, marketing and promotion of your business may require a more lavish approach. However the entrepreneur should demand proof of a direct correlation between this type of expense and revenue generated.

The amount spent on charitable donations is a very sensitive area. Robert Allen and other successful businessmen recommend that 10 percent of income be set aside for donations. However, the individual entrepreneur may decide that his working capital is too tight for cash donations. In that case the entrepreneur may consider donating his time, or production, or an equivalent service instead of cash. Successful entrepreneurs like Andrew Carnegie waited until they had banked their wealth before doing good works. Bill Gates and Warren Buffett were worth billions before they set up their foundations.

Even with careful husbandry unexpected working capital demands may arise due to legal problems, theft, fraud, market corrections and other business risks. Therefore it is important to develop backup sources of working capital and to keep lines of communications open with bankers and lenders at all times.

SUMMARY

Entrepreneurs rarely have enough working capital and usually underestimate the amount needed to reach break-even. As a rule of thumb, it is best to double the estimate of cash required. Contingency plans should be made to secure this much larger amount of capital. Entrepreneurs should be keenly aware that money escapes from most people, and businesses, like sand between the fingers. Every penny of expense must be scrutinized. This demands a disciplined and a tough minded approach to cost control. The entrepreneur must minimize personal spending and perks. Deferred gratification is a key to start-up survival.

ACTION

Entrepreneur, ensure that you have adequate working capital and backup plans for obtaining more as the business grows or problems arise.

Working Capital

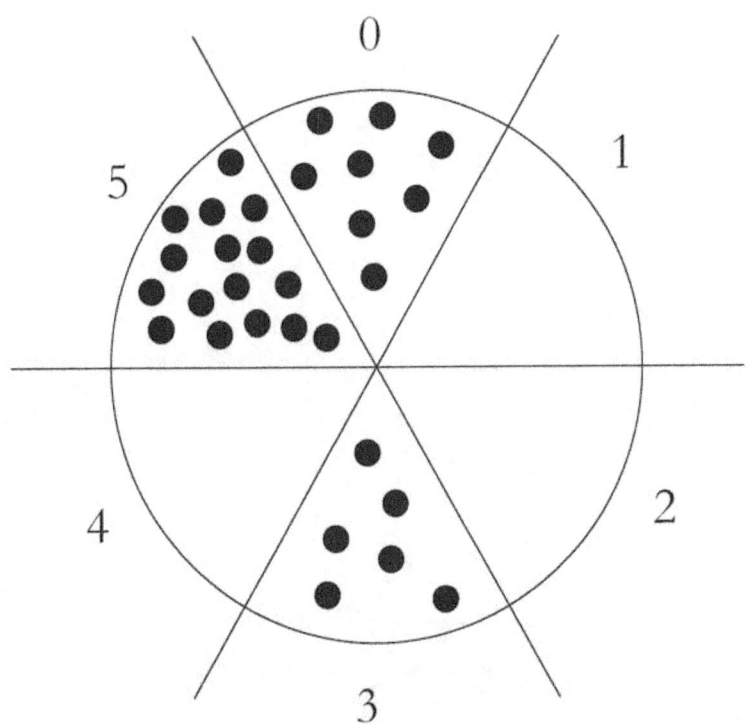

SCORING

Average score of my failures: 3.7
(adequate capital was not provided or planned for)

Average score of my successes: 1.2
(clearly I had more resources and better planning)

Your score is _____?

10

LACK OF RESPECT FOR PLANNING

Annual and long-range business planning was a responsibility of mine throughout much of my career in large corporations. Later as a consultant to start-ups and small businesses I brought the full range of my experience and critical faculties to this task of planning. However, I rarely put as much effort into planning my own start-ups. Nor have I been consistent in preparing annual reviews and updates for my own operating businesses. This is difficult to reconcile with my firm belief that business planning is critical to survival and success.

Absence of in depth planning was the case in my venture into the tanning industry. My interest was aroused by an article in a popular entrepreneurship magazine. The apparently low cost of entry was of particular importance, as I only had $15,000 – not much to start a business but that was my working capital. Without further thought, planning, training or advice I studied a list of suppliers. The more expensive tanning beds I rejected in favor of lower cost tanning booths. The assembly plant was in small town in Oklahoma. At the time, I did not realize that the primary demand was for tanning beds rather than stand-up tanning booths. When I arrived in their show room I was impressed by the number of users who streamed in and out. Not until later did I realize that they had sneakily hired a temporary receptionist and some other folk to use the booths while I was there. This gave me a false impression of the popularity and revenue generating capability of the booths.

In a few days three booths together with a supply of tanning tubes were delivered to my house. I then searched for places that would like to have them. This proved difficult but I eventually found a hair salon, a nail salon, and a fitness studio that would work with me. The plan was to share 50:50 in the revenue, but I did not have money to promote them, nor a way to audit usage. As a result the booths were underutilized and generated little revenue for me. I had no idea how to run this business and gradually grew disinterested. After a time the locations returned the booths and I put them into storage. There they languished for years until I disposed of them at a loss.

Franchisers and lenders require business plans as a matter of course. The Small Business Association and SCORE consultants are strongly in favor. Business writers in their thousands recommend the preparation of business plans. Angel investors and venture capitalist require detailed plans. In my case lack of planning has correlated with my failures and careful planning with my successes.

What is interesting is that research has not found a strong statistical correlation with failure and more research is surely required. It is a fact that small businesses, including start-ups, rarely prepare detailed business plans except when required by third parties. This lack of attention to planning has much to do with the conflict between the urgent day to day demands of the business and the less urgent thinking required by planning. Then this task may be deferred to the next day and yet the next day, until the thinking and planning required for long term survival never gets done.

There is also a degree of over confidence. We entrepreneurs like to think that we know what we are doing; where we are going, and how to get there. The frequency of failure would indicate that this is not true. In too many cases this self-delusion results in lower profits, loss of capital and non-survival.

Entrepreneurs should commence by preparing a one page plan outline of their business idea. This summary should include:

1. Short business description
2. Number of expected customers and average sale per customer
3. Revenue projection and timing of cash receipts if delayed
4. Staff required including the owner(s)
5. Cost of staff including taxes
6. Furniture, equipment and other capital expense
7. Cost of production and/or cost of outside services
8. Overhead expense, office supplies, legal, CPA and other expense
9. Total expense before contingency
10. Expense contingency of 10% (costs are always higher than you expect)
11. Total expense including contingency

12. Net cash flow (cash collected less total out of pocket by month in the first year, by quarter in the second year, and then by year for three years)

In addition to this income and expense financial planning, it's also important to detail the following:

13. Unique Selling Proposition (This concept is covered in Chapter 12)
14. Source of funds/working capital
15. Amount of funds/working capital
16. Owners experience as it relates to this business
17. Risk factors
18. Return on Investment expected

This summary should be discussed with experienced businessmen. If they consider the idea viable the entrepreneur should test for possible investment interest. If they express interest then this start-up idea may deserve further study. Failure to develop investor interest is a strong signal that you are on the wrong track and may be headed into a black hole.

To progress the business idea the entrepreneur should develop a detailed business plan. This will be 20 to 30 pages including:

1. Title Page: company name, business address, phone number, email and web-site.
2. Executive summary: This captures the essence of the plan in 1-3 pages. It is prepared last. This is all that most people will read.
3. Table of contents: directs people to the page(s) they want to read
4. General description of the business: the big idea, goals and strategy
5. Product/Service description: important attributes of the product or service and the benefits to the customers.

6. Market description: market research summary, projected growth, expert opinion.
7. Competition: strengths and weaknesses, market share, profit levels.
8. Marketing and selling strategy: resources required, Unique Selling Proposition, distribution channels, how to persuade customers to buy. Lack of planning in this area is a serious weakness in most plans.
9. (For manufacturing companies): How and where to produce and ensure quality.
10. Organization, partners and management: functional responsibility and short resumes of key personnel.
11. Board of Directors: Must include people with relevant experience and skills.
12. Financial Plan: This is a key part. Avoid being over-optimistic. Match but do not expect to undercut industry margins. Cash flow, balance sheet and income statements and capital expense estimates. Best guess, high side, and low side range will help.
13. Present ownership: Investors and corporate format - C Corp, S Corp, LLC or Limited Partnership etc.
14. Capitalization plan: How much money to raise that is consistent with cash flow forecasts; in accordance with terms and conditions for loans and equity participation.
15. Return to investors: What return should they expect and the projected timing of a public offering or repayment of debt.

16. Assumptions and risks: Alternative strategies if the original assumptions are wrong. Backup plan if primary sources of capital disappear, major problems arise or customers do not materialize. *The need to activate Plan B so the start-up can survive and grow occurs more often than even experienced businessman expect.*

17. Supporting material: Brochures, magazine articles, technical papers, market research studies and references.

Once this plan is approved then the entrepreneur will move ahead to build the business. Progress against plan should be evaluated on a regular basis perhaps monthly or quarterly. This process is an important owner/investor management tool. Annually results are compared to plan and a new plan prepared with as much detail as possible. At a minimum this should be one page long consisting of a comparison to the original one page plan outline.

While not ideal the use of a short form approach may encourage overwhelmed and over-stressed entrepreneurs to take time to plan. This is similar to a sea captain studying charts or a hiker scrutinizing a map to determine location and route on a journey. Once that is established an intelligent decision may be made as to where to go next.

In start-up planning the entrepreneur should consider SWOT analysis (this approach is credited to Albert S. Humphrey, a management consultant who worked at the Stanford Research Institute). A SWOT analysis consists of outlining the:

1. Strengths of,
2. Weaknesses of,
3. Opportunities for, and
4. Threats to the business.

Also a second SWOT analysis should be prepared from a competitor's viewpoint. This important idea is discussed in the book *All I Really Need to Know in Business I Learned at Microsoft* by Julie Bick. This SWOT assumes a dynamic market place in which competitors actively respond to loss of market share. They may make price, advertising and/or product changes. The start-up will need to change and adjust to the actions of its competitors. This process continues in waves of action and response as long as the business exists.

SUMMARY

Start-ups are often not well planned. However, entrepreneurs should prepare and test business plans before going far with their start-ups. Once in business they should prepare annual plans and monitor results against plan. This process increases the probability of arriving at their intended destination. It is important to consider how existing competitors will respond to the start-up. These actions improve the chance of survival and success.

ACTION

Develop a one page summary of your business idea. Have this reviewed by experienced businessmen and possible investors. Then develop a detailed business plan including SWOT analyses.

Business Planning

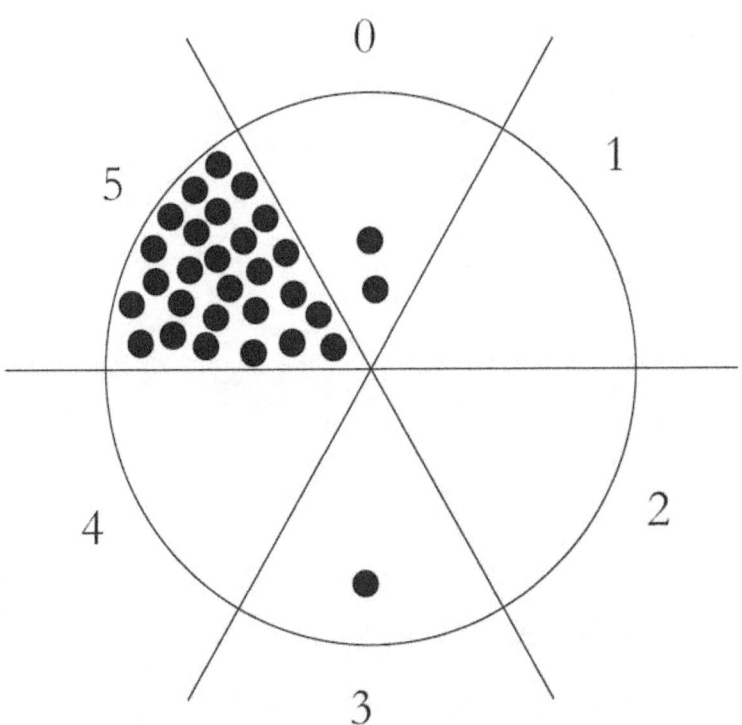

SCORING

Average score of my failures: 5.0
(Good grief! - what was I going on in my mind?)

Average score of my successes: 2.6
(better, but still not good enough.)

Your score is _____?

11

NON-USE OF PROJECT PLANNING AND CONTROL

Project planning and control is an important tool in managing the implementation of a start-up. It dovetails nicely with a comprehensive business plan though there are some areas of overlap. While I had extensive experience in using this technique as an executive, I was guilty of rarely considering it in my own start-ups.

In my first management position, I was responsible for computer operations at a nationally known bank. My boss, the Vice President in charge of Administration, was an emaciated worrier on his second heart attack. He kept a "To Do List" on the back of a punch card in the inside pocket of his suit jacket. Recently arrived from England, I still wore removable shirt collars and used steel sprung arm bands on my shirt sleeves. These were originally designed to keep shirt cuffs clean and out of ink wells! Despite the image problem, I managed to pick up quite a bit about the emerging world of information technology.

My first major task was to coordinate conversion to a new generation of computers. For this I developed a project planning, scheduling and control procedure to monitor the delivery and installation of each piece of equipment. When target dates were missed my frustration boiled over and I would berate the vendor's salesman over his broken promises. In his white laundered shirt, stripped tie, tailored suit, and highly polished shoes he listened carefully, kept his temper, made new promises and still failed to deliver on time.

Although many parts arrived late I brought the project in on schedule. This was primarily due to detailed planning, recognition of task inter-dependencies, close follow-up and the application of extra human resources to catch up as necessary.

Even today, from 50% to 90% of projects are delivered late and over budget in areas as different as information systems, new products and construction. Cost was underestimated in almost 90% of projects - roads by 20%, tunnels and bridges by 34%, and railways by 45% in a study by Flyvbjerg, Holm and Buhl - *How common and how large are cost overruns in transport infrastructure projects*. The authors noted that percentage overruns increase with the size of a project and that the accuracy of estimates has not improved over the years.

From the bank, I was head-hunted by a Fortune 500 company. At their corporate headquarters I developed a computer systems project planning and control system. This was based on that used by the military for the Distant Early Warning System. (The DEW System was developed during the Cold War to provide early warning of a potential Soviet bomber attack.)

For start-up project planning and control, I recommend a four phase approach that progresses the original idea along a development path until the business opens. The phases are:

Phase 1 Concept

This phase consists of a brief description of the business, the market to be served, the revenue potential, development cost, operating cost, and, resources needed in terms of people, equipment, supplies, and inventory. The financing/capital required and the possible sources of capital are outlined. A guestimate is made of when sales will begin and when break-even will occur. Finally, there should be a statement of the risks and other factors for decision-making. Next the entrepreneur should arrange a review by trusted advisors and businessmen with experience in the market and industry. Based on this review, the entrepreneur and his advisors should make a formal decision to go on to the next phase or drop the idea. This Phase is similar to the one page plan outline discussed in the preceding chapter.

Phase 2: Analysis

This consists of an analysis and detailed description of the business, market research and marketing plan, production plan, sales plan, financial plan, capital investment plan, funding plan, timeline, risk analysis, head count plan, business structure, and licenses and permits required.

At the conclusion of this work the entrepreneur again conducts a review with professionals and experts. Then a formal decision is made to either stop or proceed to the next phase.

Phase 3 Detailed Specifications

The detailed specification phase takes the Phase 2 material and breaks it down into as much detail as possible. There should be an evaluation with experts, fellow businessmen, and trusted advisors. While a start-up is not usually a life or death experience, entrepreneurs should be as tenacious and tough-minded in project planning and control as were the generals and staffs involved in Operation Overlord under General Eisenhower in 1944.

This phase is complete when a final plan is prepared and approved by the entrepreneur's board of advisors. Company funding should be resolved as part of this phase.

Phase 4: Implementation

The task in Phase 4 is to develop a schedule: secure funding, hire staff, find space, acquire production and office equipment, develop systems and procedures, develop and test prototypes, make revisions, build product and commence sales. All of this is conducted under a detailed implementation plan with dates, resources and responsibilities assigned.

In the case of a retail store Phase 4 proceeds from the Phase 3 decision to set up the business. Following this the entrepreneur would lease premises, decide on layout, define the opening inventory, search for staff, and hire contractors and suppliers. The project management process would continue with work coordination, financing, bank account opening, incorporation, hiring of lawyers and accountants, advertising and promotion, and all the other steps needed before opening the doors to customers. When the doors open Phase 4 and the project plan are complete. From that point day to day operations begin.

A good project plan will lead to more accurate budgeting, scheduling, time management and performance. The better the project plan, the fewer the slips in the implementation schedule and in cost overruns.

During day to day operations, project planning and control is a useful tool and may be effectively employed when opening a new branch, launching a new product or introducing a new marketing plan. These changes are material, and their implementation and effectiveness will be enhanced by applying the Four Phase method. This will help ensure the appropriate consideration, review and implementation of any changes to the original business plan and model.

On at least three start-ups, in which I did not follow the project planning method, I also did not have firm criteria to avoid project creep. As key performance dates and targets were missed, I provided or obtained additional funding to allow time for implementation. In the process, I convinced myself that this would solve the problem. Of course, I incurred further losses as a result.

A missed date or missed commitment by a vendor, contractor, debtor or employee is a signal to the wise not to throw good money after bad. The same goes for any project or investment. The supplicant (project manager, sub-contractor, builder, wife or child) may have a plausible story, make promises galore and make a plea that will wrench your heart strings. Stand firm! Second chances require someone else's money, time and energy!

SUMMARY

Project planning and control methodology is widely used in corporate America. Most methods have at least four phases: concept, analysis, detailed specification and implementation. In best practice, each phase ends with a formal review and sign off. Entrepreneurs who apply project planning and control to their start-ups and operating business will save time and money. They will also reduce their risk of failure.

ACTION

Develop a project implementation plan for your start-up. Then work the plan in a disciplined manner.

Project Planning & Control

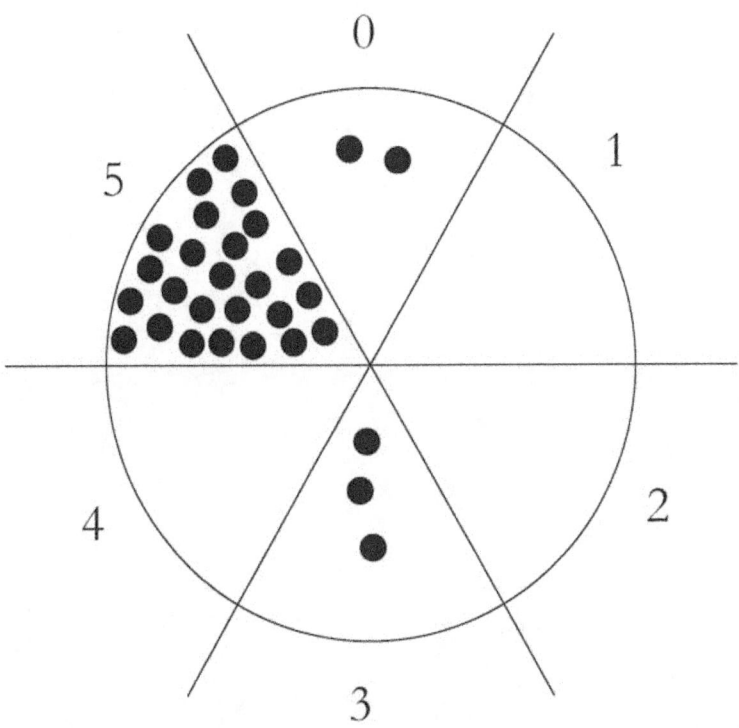

SCORING

Average score of my failures: 4.8
(virtually no project planning at all)

Average score of my successes: 1.8
(much better)

Your score is _____?

12

WEAK USP, SALES AND MARKETING

Every business needs a Unique Selling Proposition (USP); but, a start-up needs one as a thirsty traveler in a desert needs water.

The USP concept sets your product or service apart from others that may be on the market. It gives potential customers a reason to pay attention to you – the new kid on the block. With a USP, your product or service has an edge that helps you to survive and grow.

If you do not have a USP then you are virtually doomed to extinction!

Consider a mongoose facing a cobra. On the one hand, you have a six foot, coiled, malicious killer with lethal, poisonous fangs. On the other hand, you have a small mammal with sharp teeth and pure concentration. Who will win this battle to the death?

Based on size, you might place a wager on the cobra. But the savvy, informed bet is that the mongoose will dash in and snap the snake's neck at the speed of lightning—avoiding in mid-air the counter strike of the snake. Or at least that's the idea!

Like the mongoose, the entrepreneur must have a USP that provides speed and agility to avoid the counter-strike of the established competition. This is the type of USP that will give the entrepreneur's baby a chance to survive the oppressive marketing power and deep pockets of established competitors.

Jay Abraham displayed a deep understanding of USP in *Your Marketing Genius at Work*: To quote and abridge his work: "USP is that distinct and appealing idea that sets you and your business apart from every other 'me too' competitor."

Some of Jay's examples of USP statements are:

1. "Most service companies work from 9 to 5. Ours works 24 hours a day."
2. "Most HVAC contractors handle one or two manufacturing brands. We offer ten brands."
3. "If you are in the market for X product, then check our competitor Y. Then check our price. We guarantee to be at least 20% lower."
4. "Your money back, if you can find a lower price from our competitors."

Your USP should be simple enough to include on business cards, letterheads, direct mail, web pages and into every form of marketing you use. As a matter of consistent practice your start-up should furnish the prospect with plenty of examples of how you deliver your USP. This message should be repeated again and again through frequent promotions. On a consistent basis the start-up should ask satisfied customers for referrals, and ask dissatisfied customers to give them a chance to make good.

Early in the planning process, the start-up entrepreneur should decide on a USP, have experts review and confirm this decision, and then test the idea before launching the new business. One approach is to ask potential customers if they would buy the service or product should it become available. Why spend time, energy and money on an idea, without finding out if there is enough market demand, to make the venture worthwhile?

SUMMARY

Many start-ups do not have a Unique Selling Proposition, and do not pre-test their ideas before substantial time and expense is committed. Market testing plays a vital role in the development of a competitive product. A USP provides a marketing edge that will help generate sales and profits.

ACTION

Entrepreneur, write down your USP in less than twenty words. Then test the response of potential customers to your USP.

USP, Sales & Marketing

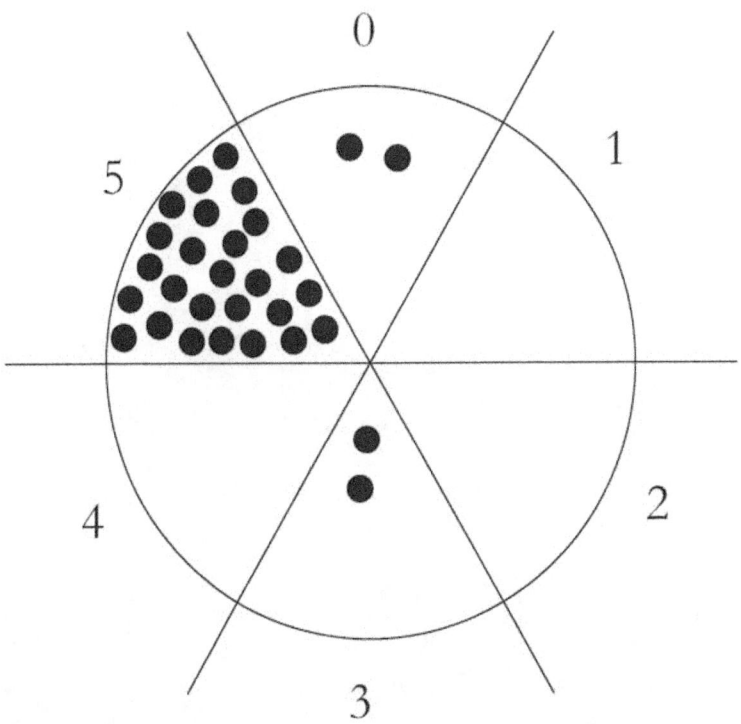

SCORING

Average score of my failures: 5.0
(this was a material factor in the failure of my efforts)

Average score of my successes: 2.2
 (an improvement but miles to go yet)

Your score is _____?

13

INADEQUATE ACCOUNTING KNOWLEDGE

The Sumerians developed the earliest known writing around 4000 B.C. They also had a method of recording the quantity of grain bought, sold and stored. Mankind has understood the importance of accurate record keeping from the earliest times.

Accounting is fundamental to business success. So it is surprising that some entrepreneurs consider that strong operations, product and sales knowledge – but not knowledge of accounting – are sufficient to start a business. They underestimate the importance of having a good grasp of accounting principles. Without it, they are not in full control of their new business.

Dare I say that most entrepreneurs are familiar with the Profit and Loss Statement? They monitor revenues by product line and expenses on a regular basis. Some extroverted entrepreneurs will crow about how much they made last month. But nearly every entrepreneur has little understanding of the balance sheet and cash flow. Yet these two statements are of equal or greater importance.

At the simplest level, the balance sheet shows the assets, liabilities and net equity of the business. Changes here can result in business failure even if the income statement is in positive territory and the business is profitable.

The assets side includes - cash in banks, accounts receivable, inventory, deposits, investments, land and buildings, machinery and equipment, tools, office equipment and other assets.

The liabilities side includes accounts payable, credit card obligations, taxes owed, short term loans, and long term loans like mortgages.

The equity section shows the original equity investment, additional paid in capital, retained earnings and current period earnings or losses.

The profit and loss statement and the balance sheet should be prepared monthly. Then the entrepreneur should spend time comparing the results against the financial budget.

Once the balance sheet is fully understood, entrepreneurs should direct their attention to the third type of financial statement— the cash flow statement.

The surest way for the non-accounting entrepreneur to understand cash flow is to prepare one. "What!" you may exclaim. "That is crazy. I am an entrepreneur not a bookkeeper!"

Let me put it this way – the entrepreneur who does not understand a specific function of his business has a blind spot, and the more the blind spots, the higher the likelihood of failure. So, entrepreneur, pull up your sleeves and get to work.

The first step is to obtain balance sheets from dates that are a year or a month apart. Then the amounts for each period are deducted from each other for every line item. These changes are the components of cash flow for that period of time. For a small start-up, and for planning purposes, a spreadsheet program such as Excel may be used. This helps align the accounts, and calculate the changes. Skill in using Excel or similar spreadsheet programs is a basic requirement of entrepreneurship.

In the early months and years of a start-up, assets such as inventory and accounts receivable may grow substantially. Also the business will need computers, telephones, operating equipment and space to operate in. All these cost money which must be balanced by an increase in accounts payable, credit card debt, loans, mortgages, or owner capital. If the start-up is profitable, an increase in retained earnings may also provide a source of cash for the business. The important thing to understand is that an increase in the assets side of the balance sheet constitutes a <u>USE</u> of cash, and an increase in the liabilities and equity side constitutes a <u>SOURCE</u> of cash.

While counter-intuitive, the retention of cash in bank accounts constitutes a use of cash. Don't think you are alone if you find this a bit difficult to grasp. After all, we all like to have a nice sum in the bank, especially if this is the result of after tax profits. However an increase in the cash on hand must be balanced by an increase in the liabilities and equity side of the balance sheet.

Accounts payable is an important source of cash, as vendors have loaned the business money, by providing products and services, without having been paid yet. However if payments are excessively delayed then the suppliers may withdraw credit and demand accelerated payment. This is the worst possible situation to be in and frequently precedes the demise of the business.

Financial statements prepared by CPAs often include funds flow statements. These statements are prepared according to sophisticated and frequently changing accounting rules. In general these are less useful to the entrepreneur than a cash flow analysis that shows balance sheet changes as discussed above.

The topic and implications of cash flow analysis is further covered in Chapter 2 *Negative Cash Flow*, and Chapter 9 *Shortage of Working Capital*.

The entrepreneur who does not have experience in accounting should follow a course of study to rectify this situation. Time spent understanding balance sheets, profit and loss statements, and cash flow will be highly beneficial in the survival and eventual success of the startup.

SUMMARY

Many entrepreneurs have little knowledge of accounting beyond a simple Profit and Loss Statement. However, Balance Sheet and Cash Flow Statement understanding is of equal or greater importance. Entrepreneurs planning to make their start-ups successful will grit their teeth and learn this side of the business. They will bring themselves to a level of competence and comfort with accounting reports. *Accounting is NOT beyond the ability of the ordinary mind to comprehend!*

ACTION

Make sure you receive and understand the three types of financial statements. Pay special attention to the Balance Sheet and to the Cash Flow Statement.

Accounting Knowledge

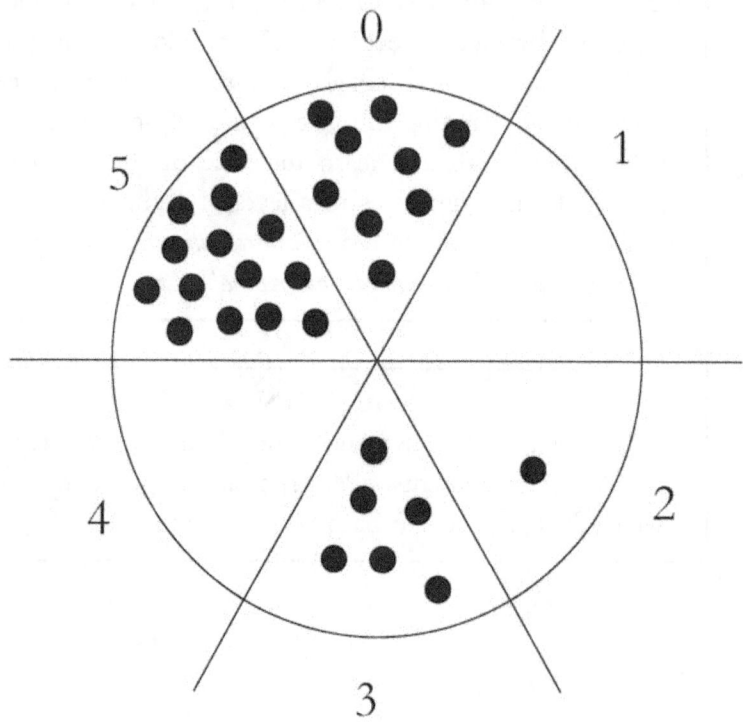

SCORING

Average score of my failures: 3.5 (I had the skills but not the discipline to use them)

Average score of my successes: 0.6 (this should have been zero but is still pretty good)

Your score is _____?

14

HIRING THE WRONG PEOPLE AND FAILING TO FIRE THEM

The famous (or infamous) GE directive to fire the bottom 10% performers every year was a very blunt instrument. The process was called "Differentiation" whereby employees were divided into the top performing 20%, the vital middle 70% and the bottom 10%. The bottom performers were those who could not get the job done and needed to go, according to Jack Welch's in *Jack, Straight from the Gut.*

In a start-up non-performers may have a greater impact than in a large company because there is less room for error. In a small business every individual must perform competently or failure becomes more likely. For my part I subscribe to the mantra "fire the worst and hire the best." This means that as the bottom performers are dismissed, their replacements should be able to perform at the highest level, thereby raising the average performance level in leaps and bounds.

As a corporate executive, I found that I could quickly identify underperformers when I first encountered them. What I needed to do was promptly arrange for their dismissal or transfer. If I did not move quickly, I would find myself living with quirks and non-performance.

Worse still, I would waste time coaching, training and motivating them to improve their performance. This was mostly an ineffective use of my time. What I needed to do was study my employees and when they were more of a liability than an asset I needed to bite the bullet and fire them.

Employee performance problems can occur in any position and with any employee. In fact, it may be more common (and certainly cause more difficulties) near the top of an organization due to executive privilege. As a workout specialist and consultant, I ran into a lot of deadwood at the executive level in the companies that I advised. These incompetents had to be pruned so that the mid-level managers, or sergeants as I would think of them, could keep the company running. In the main, the sergeants knew how to get the job done. Frequently the higher-ups gave incorrect or confusing instructions and wasted the sergeants' time with unnecessary meetings and bureaucracy. Only when the red ink was stopped was it possible to seek out new marketing executives and other key personnel, including a new CEO to lead the organization to the next level.

In my experience, the mantra "Leopards don't change their spots" applies equally to employees. In general, employees who are not action oriented, or are frequently absent, or play games on their computers, or have a bad attitude, or make mistakes and generally underperform, will continue this behavior whatever you do.

While it is important to aim to keep turnover low, there is a right way and a wrong way to go about it. You don't want to do this by retaining employees who are liabilities. Instead, work on the other end: keep turnover low by emphasizing employee selection, the hiring process, training, coaching and support. This reduces the time required to hire and train new employees and minimizes work disruption.

The most important criteria in hiring employees for a start-up are:

1. Specific job experience - so they need little training,
2. Worked in a small business before,
3. History of steady growth and success,
4. Not a job hopper,
5. Have defined life goals,
6. Have excellent references,
7. Are geographically stable.

In many of my start-ups I did not invest enough time in employee selection. Too often my employees turned out to be poor performers, drug users and thieves. Don't let that happen to you!

Ross Perot had an expression that he used to inspire and build a great team, when he first started Electronic Data Systems. This expression was: "Eagles don't flock. You have to find them one at a time." To find outstanding employees the entrepreneur needs a wide base of candidates. These must be scrutinized, interviewed, and tested for pertinent skills and compatibility to find the absolute best one. In a business of less than 50 employees, the chief executive officer should be closely involved in the hiring process and must provide the final approval.

Cesar Millan, in his TV show *"The Dog Whisperer"*, nudges dogs to distract them. He then gives them immediate and consistent feedback. At the same time he trains the dog's owners by showing them the right method and correcting the humans immediately as well! The entrepreneur should use this type of immediate and consistent feedback, coaching and timely correction of employee performance where necessary.

A useful tool for the entrepreneur is "Management by Objectives" (MBO) as outlined by Peter Drucker in his book *The Practice of Management.* Under MBO each employee is assigned objectives that align with the company business plan. The expectation is that the objectives will become personal goals that people want to achieve for themselves. The underlying concept is that people are self-motivated and want to contribute and to accomplish the assigned objectives. In employee performance MBO is considered more effective than management by domination, management by control and micro-management. While many entrepreneurs employ the latter styles of management successfully, the MBO style is preferable; especially in building a business that will run profitably in the entrepreneur's absence. (The creation of a sustainable business is discussed further in Chapter 20.)

Combining immediate feedback and coaching with MBO and annual reviews will ensure that employees are monitored, held to a high standard, rewarded on a timely basis, and fired if they do not perform. Successful entrepreneurs will develop and implement such a system.

In all interactions with employees the entrepreneur should ensure there is an open and fair discussion, with the entrepreneur spending much of the time listening. Differences of opinion, if properly handled, will improve understanding of performance expectations and the support that the employee needs to do the work.

On new hires the 90 day window after hiring must be adhered to. Weekly and monthly reviews should take place exactly on time.

If turnover is high the entrepreneur should carefully review the hiring and training process to see where the problem lies. Other factors to consider are clarity of company mission, objectives, instructions, procedures and systems. These may need upgrading and improving to support employee performance.

In the end, if you keep hiring duff employees, *you* are the problem, so keep firing them until you get the process right (and get professional personnel management help). Don't worry about the cost of state and federal unemployment insurance because of high turnover. It's less than the cost of hiring the wrong people! Instead, concentrate on learning how to improve the process.

SUMMARY

Entrepreneurs should strive to find and hire top quality employees, and quickly fire underperformers. If this is done the workforce will be more productive, and the entrepreneur will have more time to service customers and develop the business. The lowest performing 10% should be fired annually to be replaced with top performers.

ACTION

Find, hire, and train the best people possible for your new venture. Install a MBO system and promptly fire non-performers.

Hiring the Wrong People & Failing to Fire Them

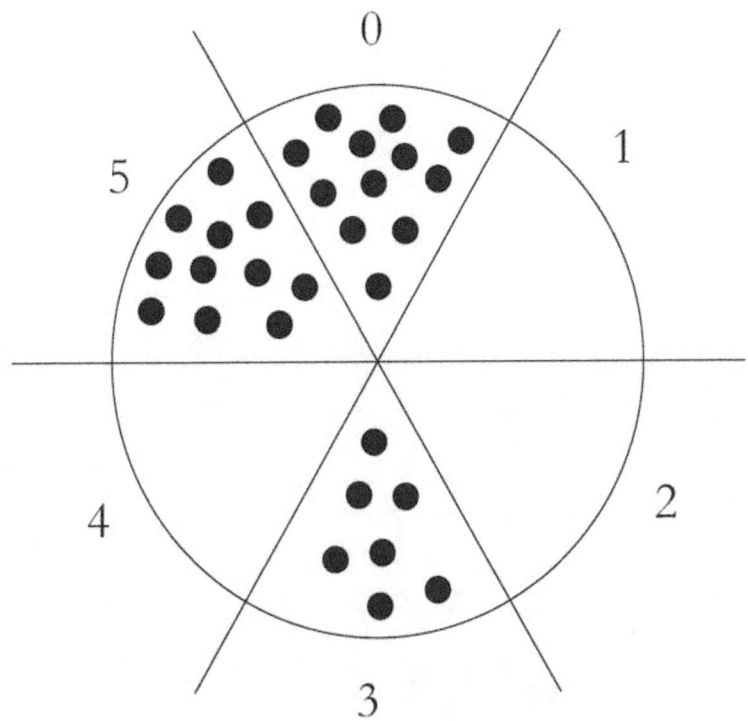

SCORING

Average score of my failures: 2.7
(middle level performance)

Average score of my successes: 1.8
(improving personnel management paid off)

Your score is _____?

15

NEGATIVE ECONOMY

Unfortunately, in addition to all of the factors leading to business failure that the entrepreneur can control, there are some that the entrepreneur can't control at all. That makes taking care of the other factors all the more important. Even if you do everything right, you can sometimes fail. There isn't a whole lot of room for error!

The U.S. economy goes from boom time to bust every few years. Sometimes as in the 1930s, and the period since 2007, the decline is very steep, unemployment rises, and business conditions are very difficult. The impact on start-ups and small business can be devastating. The effect on individual businesses may be mitigated or worsened by multiple factors including location, type of industry and strength of customers.

During the financial crisis, I received the bad news that the bank that had made us a land development loan had gone bust. The "us" in this case was an entity that I co-owned with a long term partner. The acquiring bank placed our loan in their workout department. The VP in charge ignored our financial strength and good payment history. Immediate payment in full was demanded. To keep them at bay, we provided new Personal Financial Statements, agreed to a partial pay down and provided copies of lease customer contracts that would support continuing development. "Not interested," they said. "However, we will renew the loan for six months at a time." At each renewal we had to go through the same rigmarole with closing costs, legal fees and partial pay downs. Finally they gave us a two-year ultimatum to take our business elsewhere or face foreclosure!" Of course, since the whole banking system was in crisis, there were precious few lenders willing to make a land loan. So there we were, stuck at zero, making payments on a no money earning asset. Luckily, we had deep enough pockets that we were able to hold on until we could secure a payoff loan. Such are the problems that small businesses may face when the economy turns negative.

Another problem area for small business is government action. At federal, state and local levels, new laws, rules, regulations and taxes appear with disheartening frequency. Small business is both impeded, and to a degree helped, by congressional efforts to satisfy lobbyists, but in general, the harm outweighs the help. Big business is especially effective at influencing legislation. They are the recipients of corporate welfare that helps their profits often at the expense of small businesses. It is necessary to look no further than aid and subsidies provided to the oil industry, real estate, agriculture and most recently the massive efforts to prop up banks that were judged "too big to fail."

At a state and local level, big business is often "bribed" to relocate by reduced real estate taxes, sales tax and/or other fees. Expense reductions such as these are not made available to a flower shop start-up. The argument that the flower shop gains custom with the arrival of a new plant, for example, is rarely valid. Overall, small business would derive greater benefit if there was less distortion to natural economic growth because of state competitive bidding for new industry and plants. What benefits the economy, of say, North Carolina, does so at the expense of small business, in say, Michigan.

Generally big business has an advantage over small business when choosing a new location for expansion to take advantage of such offers. However with a new start-up, the entrepreneur may be more flexible as to location. Texas today has a steady economy, while in the 1980s the Savings and Loan debacle knocked the Texas economy flat on its back. In general, the entrepreneur should consider a city or town where the economy is balanced and not dependent on one industry. This will help cushion the new business from the vagaries of the business cycle.

State and local government also may cause problems for the start-up through rezoning or road improvement. Perhaps a hair salon start-up provided licensed massage therapy as well. Then a new ordinance is passed that "massages" are not allowed within one half mile of a school or church. The reduced revenue might put the hair salon owner out of business.

Another example of government action which can impact a small business would be a road widening project that hindered customer access to local businesses. Near my house a through road has been half closed for six months due to the construction of a new bridge. This has caused a serious decline in trade for the barbecue restaurant on the corner. Perhaps the restaurant should have been aware of the DOT plans, but this is not possible in all cases. This type of unexpected interruption of business can cause the failure of even well-run businesses. The cost of congressional and state attempts at social engineering include labor hours, minimum wage, worker compensation, health, and disability laws. While some of these laws remedy abuses, the cost of compliance is a burden that small business may have difficulty meeting.

To paraphrase the first paragraph in this chapter: As the owner of a start-up business your success or failure often depends on factors over which you have no control. For that reason, managing the factors that you *can* control is all the more important.

SUMMARY

The success or failure of a start-up is influenced by factors in the larger economy over which the entrepreneur has little or no control. A business can fail simply because it opens at the wrong time or in the wrong location. Lobbying by big business may influence laws that benefit them at the expense of small business. This is the world the entrepreneur inhabits. To minimize risk the entrepreneur must concentrate on doing a great job on the factors that can be controlled.

ACTION

Consider the overall state of the economy and especially in your specific location. Are there factors and knowable government plans that may help or hinder your business?

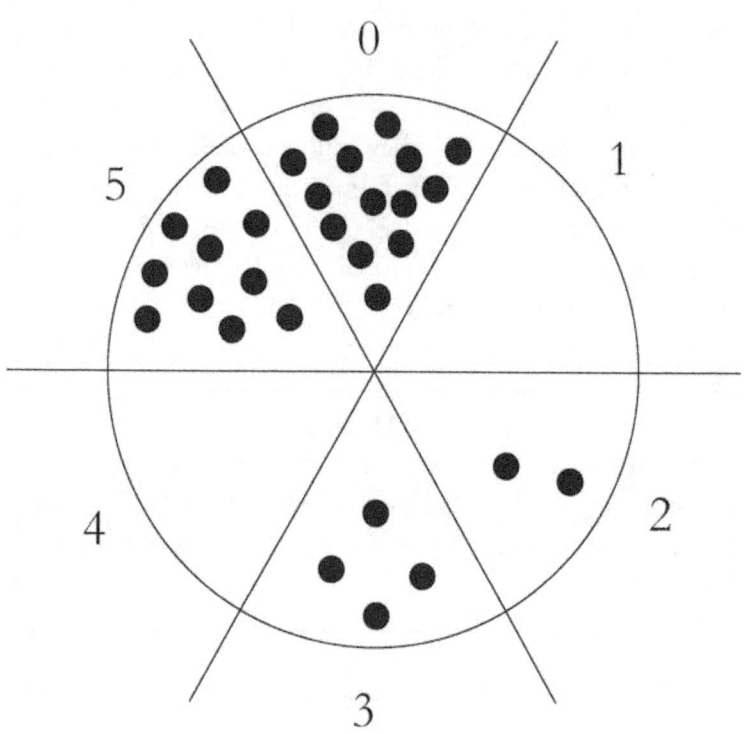

Negative Economy

SCORING

Average score of my failures: 2.4
(generally ok, but not great economic conditions)

Average score of my successes: 1.4
(no problem here)

Your score is _____?

16

LACK OF A RELEVANT EDUCATION

Far too often entrepreneurs lack the type of education that they really need to succeed in a start-up. The entrepreneur may have devoted years to school and college; in the acquisition of knowledge and skills that have little relevance to the task of making a start-up successful. This is, perhaps surprisingly also true of the curricula offered in prestigious schools of business administration. To suppose that you have the knowledge you need, because you have acquired an MBA, or have had a career in business management at the corporate level, is a serious mistake.

My English grammar school education was thorough and useful for beginning jobs in the business world. However the bachelor's degree I earned at the London School of Economics had little direct value. Among subjects like Medieval Economic History, European History, Political Philosophy, Economics and Comparative Government, only

Statistics was directly relevant. However the intensity of the studies, essays, lectures and seminars did train me to assimilate and organize the flood of information that bombards a businessman daily.

After college I took a Diploma in Management Studies course at night school and gained more practical knowledge of accounting, law, marketing and personnel management. I also took a course in Methods Study at the Cranfield Institute of Technology. There I was introduced to Gilbreth, Taylor, time-lapse photography, the psychology of change, the logic of organization, and, the improvement of manufacturing and office processes. This had direct application to my position at the time in the Organization and Methods Department at AEI-Hotpoint.

Later in the United States, I worked at Xerox, which had an excellent management development program. One of the best courses was *Effective Listening Skills*. Another was *Management Discussion Skills*. Both of these I have found useful throughout my career.

My formal education was completed with an MBA from Nova University in Florida. I accomplished this through a two-year program of weekend seminars and evening study. One of the courses was on entrepreneurship but little of what I learned helped me with my own start-ups. While I am proud of my MBA, I concur with the words of Robert Townsend author of *Up the Organization:* "By design the 'B-School' trains a senior officer class that is missing fundamental requirements for success: humility; respect for people on the firing line; deep understanding of the nature of the business, and the kind of people who can enjoy themselves making it prosper...."

The minimum requirement for the potential entrepreneur is a high school or college education that encompasses verbal and mathematical skills. In effect, the best basis is the old teacher curriculum of 'rithmetic, 'riting and reading – skills which are useful in any area of life. This should be followed by more advanced classroom study of business functions such as selling, marketing, finance, accounting, law, manufacturing, distribution, management and entrepreneurship.

After completing formal schooling the budding entrepreneur should become an apprentice in a successful small business. This experience should include detail and management level experience in each business function. Lastly, and perhaps most importantly, to maximize his chances of success, the entrepreneur should buy into this business or start one in the same industry. This is a truly realistic approach to preparing the entrepreneur for success in a small business. This approach is similar to the old fashioned parent child training in hunting, farming and specialized trades. Where this is not possible (for example in new and fast moving technologies) then the entrepreneur should actively seek out mentors and leading experts to provide training and guidance.

My start-up failures occurred in spite of the effort I made to learn everything I could about management and business methods. My real education did not begin until I acquired experience in the operation and management of real live down-to-earth businesses.

Small business owners, who attain success, tend to have achieved this because they stuck to one business in which they became an expert. In effect, they earned the equivalent of a PhD in that business. Whether they could teach others is a different matter, but they will have an in-depth understanding and competence that should be respected, if not admired. If entrepreneurs do not acquire this level of expertise then their employees and professional advisors must compensate for this. If the start-up is successful then the entrepreneur will reap the reward that comes from bringing the team together.

Even when the entrepreneur achieves his first business success, he will always be learning and improving. There's no end to it. Entrepreneurs should think of themselves as athletes who keep training and upgrading their skills and capabilities to stay on top of their game.

The entrepreneur who has grown up around small business, or has worked in one, has an innate appreciation of the requirements. He will know of the numerous tasks and skills which must be mastered. The corporate employee rarely attains this breadth of experience and understanding because his work experience is more concentrated. After a career in which secretaries had organized my office, arranged meetings, done the travel arrangements and handled the mail and telephone calls, I could not even operate a copying machine, when I went into business for myself.

I would be remiss if I did not mention that the Small Business Administration produces many reports, develops teaching material, and holds seminars that are of great value to the start-up entrepreneur. The SBA also provides financing and guarantees for bank loans in certain circumstances.

The non-profit corporation SCORE (Counselors to America's Small Business), also provides mentors, workshops and seminars for entrepreneurs. Other sources of support include the business departments of universities, and private specialized consultants and executives. Experts all over the country write books, conduct research, give lectures, provide consulting, and develop courses of study.

The budding entrepreneur should reap as much benefit as possible from such resources, and from all available business books. In addition, the web is an immense resource that gives the modern entrepreneur a leg up that was not available to his predecessors.

The entrepreneur should have a life-long, self-development plan to upgrade business skills, increase industry knowledge and attain a keen understanding of modern technology.

In scoring this factor many of my start-ups are rated 5. This is because my starting operational knowledge was often slim to none. This lack of a relevant education often overwhelmed my general knowledge of business, finance and management, and was a key factor in failure.

SUMMARY

Entrepreneurs should graduate high school and have some college or equivalent technical training. To this should be added theoretical and practical training and experience in every business function. To have the best chance of start-up success the entrepreneur will serve an apprenticeship (Chapter 4) and executive training (Chapter 6) in a small business in the chosen industry or field (Chapter 3). Throughout the entrepreneur's career continuing education is essential. This will include industry matters, product knowledge, management skills and technology. Books and seminars should be consumed on a regular basis as part of an annual self-development plan.

ACTION

Entrepreneurs - work in a small business to gain a relevant education. Research and learn everything possible about how to start a business. Learn everything possible in every pertinent skill required for the particular type of business.

Relevant Education

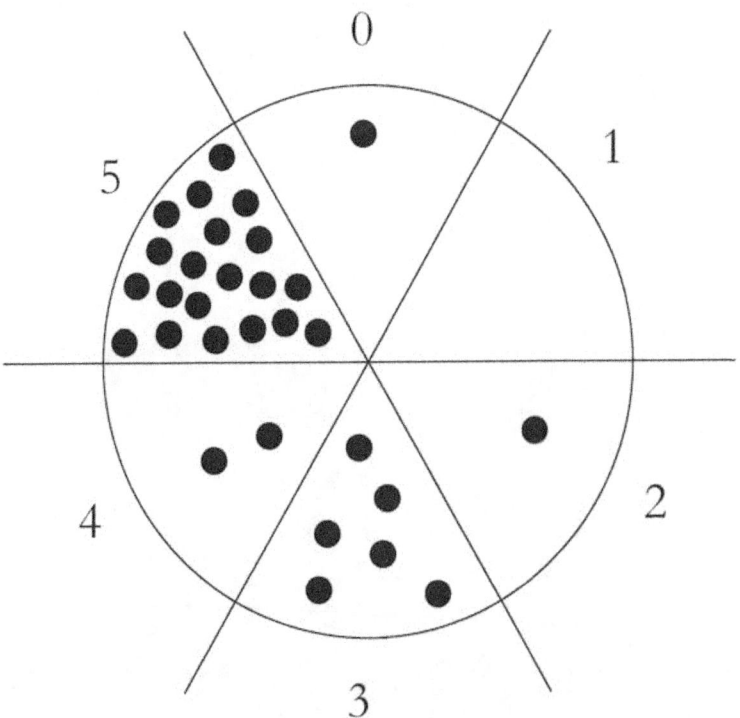

SCORING

Average score of my failures: 4.9

(really bad! I needed much more education in the operations side of the businesses)

Average score of my successes: 3.2

(operational experience gained the hard way paid off eventually!)

Your score is _____?

17

INCOMPETENT OR UNUSED
DIRECTORS OR ADVISORS

Every start-up needs experienced advisors and a Board of Directors with independent and outspoken participants. However for many years I was my own board of directors and my own advisor. This was a serious lapse in judgment and a major factor in the demise of several of my businesses.

Successful businessmen have employed me as an advisor and consultant. I have also served as a director for several companies. In that capacity the most effective company leaders have listened to my advice carefully and on many occasions profited thereby.

Why did I not do the same? The answer is in the words of Voltaire -"Is there anyone so wise as to learn by the experience of others?" In effect for many years I was simply not wise enough.

The ability to find and listen to competent advisors is a key factor in success. Advisors should be chosen on the basis of professional expertise, relevant business experience, willingness to speak truth to power, good judgment and a history of business success.

In my business of workout consultancy, I drew on my experience as a top level corporate financial executive and from my experience gained in my own start-up financial and business problems. As a result, I was able to provide effective advice in restructuring a manufacturing business, a wholesale parts business and a mini-conglomerate. I arranged the sale of assets, reduction of personnel, debt refinancing, law suit resolution, vendor negotiations and liabilities reduction.

One may wonder at how much further along I would be had I sought and listened to competent advice on my investments in businesses as distinct as temporary help, new car dealership, importing, Mexican spring water distribution, phlebotomy, tanning booths, aerial photography, antique car restoration, foreclosures, electrical contracting and immigration consulting. The wide range of different businesses and skills needed would argue for the maximum amount of expert advice, but I rarely asked anyone before charging ahead.

No matter how much you think you know about the process of starting a new business, or even how much you actually *do* know, it's a given that there are people who know things that you don't. That's even truer when the area of business you are attempting to enter is unfamiliar to you, as many of my attempts were to me. But even when the business is a familiar one to you, a different perspective can help to fill your own blind spots.

There is a famous story that explains the importance of competent advisors and experts. The premise is that there is a million dollars in your name at the top of a very high but climbable mountain. What would you do? If you thought carefully enough you would realize that you needed experts to prepare you for the climb. Then you would need an exercise program to get in top physical condition. You would need to train on hills and smaller mountains. You would need to acquire specific mountaineering skills. Then you would seek out the best and most qualified guides and equipment. With their help you would plan the route and organize the climb. The plan would involve a base camp and then more camps higher up so that you climbed in a logical and safe manner until you reached the top and claimed the prize.

Now that is the way to open a new business, and operate it successfully!!!!

SUMMARY

Wise entrepreneurs will search out and listen to competent advisors and experts. They will carefully evaluate and implement those recommendations which make sense to them. The unwise will not seek competent advice or will listen to less competent advisors. Informal or casual meetings with experts may help you make good decisions. However a better method is to create a formal board of directors and/or panel of advisors, and to consult with them regularly.

ACTION

Establish a board of directors and/or panel of advisors. Hold regular meetings with full information, and, listen carefully to their advice and recommendations.

Directors & Advisors

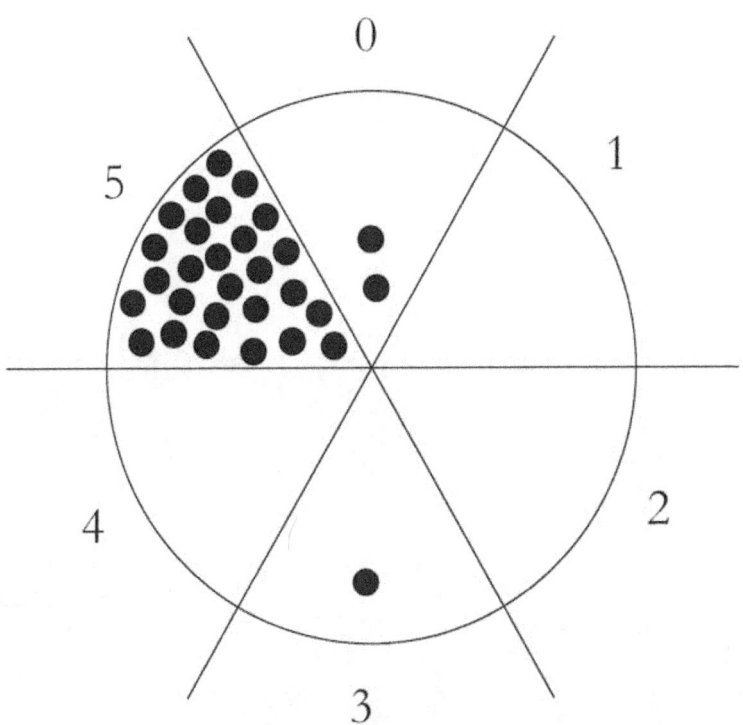

SCORING

Average score of my failures: 4.9
(this was a major and expensive reason for failure)

Average score of my successes: 2.6
(with a 0 score much greater success was possible)

Your score is _____?

18

NOT STICKING TO ONE BUSINESS

Diversification has been the downfall of many a successful business. New product lines, new locations and new markets introduce risks that frequently exceed the potential payoff. Far too often the other side of the fence looks greener. Some owners and managers are motivated by a desire to make more money or simply to have a bigger business, a macho desire if ever I heard one. Sometimes it results from boredom—with doing the same old thing, day after day. Even experienced businessmen have difficulty supervising more than one line of business. Success at one does not mean that the owner will be successful at another. Each new product line, branch or market increases the span of management control, the complexity of the business, and the level of knowledge required.

To reiterate what has been stated previously, success demands extensive knowledge of, application in, and dedication to the particular business. In other words, the successful entrepreneur becomes a specialist, and this is a key to survival and eventual success.

Unfortunately, many entrepreneurs do not understand and appreciate how their businesses became successful. In error, they attribute the success to their own genius. They downplay the participation of staff, partners and advisors. They ignore the importance of timing, circumstances, market demand and the overall state of economy. In addition they rarely place enough weight on the complexity and difficulty of adding a new line, branch or business.

In effect, they bring the day closer to an encounter with the Peter Principle. This concept was described in *The Peter Principle,* by Dr. Laurence J. Peter and Raymond Hull. This is a somewhat (but only somewhat) tongue-in-cheek theory that in a hierarchy everyone in management eventually reaches their "level of incompetence." The problem arises because good performers keep being promoted. Eventually they reach a level in the hierarchy at which they are merely competent or possibly less than competent – and there they stay, neither promoted nor fired.

To be sure, a small business is not a hierarchy, but the Peter Principle still applies, just in a different way. Successful entrepreneurs may "promote" themselves by diversifying into other ventures. Both the original business and the new venture may then underperform or even fail. Had the entrepreneur not over-extended the original business might have remained profitable and survived for many years.

Entrepreneurs would be advised to avoid excessive expansion and complication of their businesses. If growth is the plan then consider the following:

1. Internal growth derived from effective marketing and sales may require more admin personnel, changes in supply, and more working capital.
2. Product changes introduce new market dynamics and internal changes that carry their own risks.
3. As the business grows management professionals may be required displacing the start-up entrepreneur who is rarely as effective in a large business.
4. Geographical growth, adding branches and/or franchising requires a cautious approach and careful testing of the water. The use of project planning and control as outlined in Chapter 11 is recommended.
5. Plans must be updated, and decisions made, with expert guidance and board approval.

This does not mean that an entrepreneur should never embrace change. It is unusual for a business to survive for many years without adaptation as the marketplace and the economic environment change. What is essential for long term success is to concentrate on repeating what remains successful and improving every part of the business, while making the changes necessary to keep the customers satisfied.

SUMMARY

Entrepreneurs have egos that tell them they can run any type and size of business. This increases the risk that they will expand beyond their ability ("The Peter Principle.") New business lines may require different skills than those that made the entrepreneur successful in the first place. Starting one successful business is a prodigious achievement for any entrepreneur. By sticking with what they know, entrepreneurs become experts. Diversification frequently introduces unnecessary risks.

ACTION

The start-up entrepreneur should aim to stick to the one business. Then become an expert in that business.

Sticking to One Business

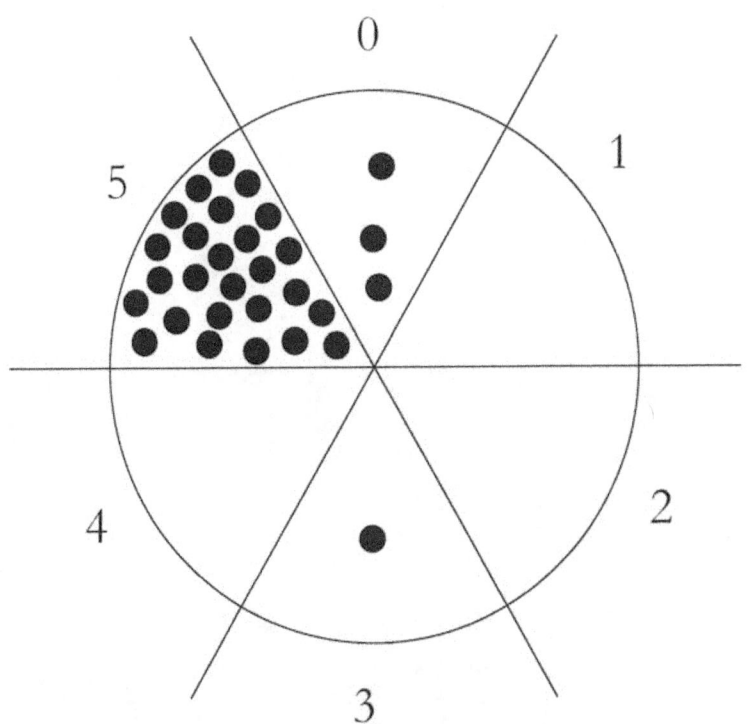

SCORING

Average score of my failures: 5.0
(I had ants in my pants and it showed)

Average score of my successes: 1.6
(much better and it showed)

Your score is _____?

19

BAD LUCK AND BLACK SWAN EVENTS

Accident and chance play a part in every life, and I have had my share! When I was twelve, a bus conductor grabbed my arm when my feet slipped off the platform as it sped around a corner. I called out "thank you" as the bus drove away. The conductor nodded and raised his eyebrows. Clearly he thought I was a typical young whippersnapper who wouldn't stay seated until the bus came to a complete stop. He was right, too. I was lucky that he was close by and alert.

Unexpected incidents happen in business as well. While preparation and perspiration and contingency plans are important, luck both good and bad, is also a key ingredient.

Every day there are rags to riches stories about entrepreneurs who owe much to circumstances and good luck. Often they enjoyed a strong economy, a time of peace, an opportunity for a good education, good health, friends, mentors, political connections, and access to start-up capital.

In Florida, hurricane and flood insurance is essential. However, when and how bad they strike is purely a matter of luck. The year after I sold an apartment building, two hurricanes severely damaged the roofs. The buyer had bought insurance with a sizable deductible that he had to cover out of his own pocket. I was spared this expense by sheer luck of timing and the buyer suffered from misfortune that was none of his own doing.

On the bad luck side, in early 2007 our land development company prepaid road improvement fees to help bridge a state/county budget timing problem. We did this to retain development rights that depended on a road-widening project. The county attorney explained that new bonds would be issued in six months, and our prepayment would be refunded, and from then on we would pay the improvement fees only as we built. However the Lehman financial crisis hit and the market for new bonds dried up. To fund the prepaid fees, we tapped our bank line of credit and were placed in a cash bind. We were unable to take advantage of the road widening project and my investment in that development was a complete write-off.

Some risks are hard to avoid – the 2011 Japanese earthquake and tsunami, for example. The loss of life, livelihoods and property was awful. This included extensive damage to atomic power plants and manufacturing. Subsequently shortages of Japanese products and parts were reported in Europe and America. These had attendant negative impacts on business in those countries as well.

In ancient Greece, the goddess Tyche presided over luck. The Romans called her Fortuna, from which comes our modern term fortune. The Japanese have the happy Buddha – Hotei. India has Lakshmi, the Hindu goddess of wealth. Even today, many people touch, rub or pray for good luck while holding a St. Christopher medallion. Both the rabbit's foot and the horseshoe were known as lucky in my family.

In his book *The Black Swan*, Nassim Taleb discussed events that occur outside the realm of normal expectations, and the ways that people concoct to view the event as logical and predictable. The title references that all swans were known as white until 1697 when black swans were found in Western Australia. The advent of the Internet, World War 1, September 11, and the BP Deepwater Horizon catastrophe may all be considered Black Swan events.

Violence, theft, robbers and riots occur almost at random. Lucky you, if you were not born in an inner city or border town where gangs and drugs are prevalent. The year of your birth may be unlucky for some. Wartime service was probably your lot if you were a 19 year old male in 1862 in America, in 1916 in England or 1940 in Germany.

War has been a constant in the history of man and can arbitrarily interrupt or destroy the works of entrepreneurs. However, great fortunes have also been built in such times. The same is true of natural disasters. Some businesses thrive during the cleanup from hurricanes while others wither and die. Recognizing this possibility, the entrepreneur will develop a contingency plan – covering the actions to take in a variety of such events.

When you are prepared you can grab good luck with both hands and maximize the opportunity. If you are unprepared then you will experience the full effect of bad luck. You will not be flexible and adaptable enough to survive the new circumstances and your start-up will fall by the wayside more often than not.

SUMMARY

Luck, both good and bad, is relevant to the success or failure of start-ups. Entrepreneurs should consider the frequency of Black Swan events and prepare contingency plans. They will then have more flexibility to adjust to sudden changes in fortune, for better or worse. When good luck shines they will be able to grab hold of the opportunity with both hands. When bad luck hits they will have more chance to adapt and survive.

ACTION

Disaster contingency planning is a critical part of survival. Expect both good and bad luck. Be ready to adapt to the opportunities and the problems that will appear like Black Swans.

Black Swan Preparation

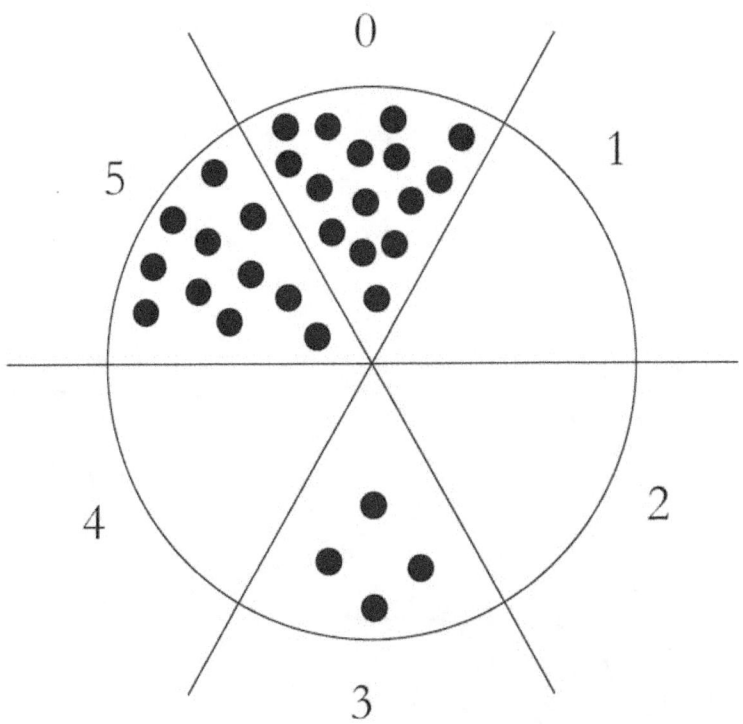

SCORING

Average score of my failures: 2.4
(bad luck played a part here)

Average score of my successes: 1.6
(much good luck and adaptability when
bad luck struck)

Your score is _____?

20

NOT BUILDING A SUSTAINABLE BUSINESS

The previous chapters have emphasized the amount of time, energy, and dedication required to start a business. Many, if not most, entrepreneurs are effectively self-employed. As such they need to keep working if the start-up is to survive. Time spent away from the business may result in lost income and possibly business failure. As long as the entrepreneur is a one man band, so to speak, this situation continues. Then when the entrepreneur retires the business must be sold or closed.

What is preferable is for the entrepreneur to think of the start-up as something that should eventually operate with only minor or at best no monitoring. That is, the business will be a self-sustaining entity. The way to do this is to think in terms of building a business system and not creating a job.

Every entrepreneur has a limited amount of time and energy to apply to the resources which have been assembled.

As the leader the entrepreneur must supervise, understand and approve all aspects of the start-up. To leverage the limited time and energy available, work should be delegated to someone else who can do it proficiently. This will allow the entrepreneur to concentrate on areas where others do not have equivalent skills.

The first step in delegation is to ruthlessly evaluate all paper work, email, snail mail, phone calls and unnecessary information consumption. These should be either eliminated or delegated.

Questions that the entrepreneur should ask include: Why do your own banking, go to the drug store, to the mall, to the office supply house or the post office? Why pay your own bills or do your own bookkeeping? Why make your own copies, clean your own floors and windows and do your own repairs? Almost always others can do these chores with equal or better efficiency. Then the entrepreneur may use this time more effectively, perhaps to search out ways to substantially increase cash flow and net worth.

The "Pareto Principle," also known as the 80-20 rule, is applicable here. Pareto, an Italian economist, observed in 1906, that 80% of the land in Italy was owned by 20% of the population. When this principle is applied to business, the expectation is that in general:

1. 80% of profits come from 20% of customers.
2. 80% of complaints come from a different set of 20% of customers.
3. 80% of sales come from 20% of the sales force.
4. 80% of profits are derived from 20% of the entrepreneur's effort.

Now let's consider an entrepreneur who aspires to build a business that will be worth a million dollars. Let us give the entrepreneur one year to do this. In that year let us have the entrepreneur work eight hours a day, five days a week for fifty weeks. This allows for two weeks' vacation and the weekends for relaxation and recovery.

In the full year the entrepreneur will work a total of 2000 hours. If the new business turns out as planned, and is operational at the end of the year, then the value of the entrepreneur's invested time is $500 per hour ($1,000,000 divided by 2000 hours).

To be worth $1 million the business should throw off a net income of $100,000 per year (after taxes, salaries and all other expenses) for at least 10 years. The value is calculated by multiplying annual net income by 10 (representing 10 years of returns.)

If the entrepreneur is active in the business, then salary paid must be included in total expense before calculating net income. However when the entrepreneur acts as an investor only, once the business is operational, then his personal earnings would not be included. The reward would be a hands-free $100,000 per year. This is the return on the invested time of one year's work (2000 hours).

To repeat and emphasize the idea: - *the objective is to build a viable business system that will operate profitably with minimum direct involvement of the entrepreneur.*

However, if the entrepreneur works in the business this time should be valued at $500. This is what the entrepreneur should earn. In addition the business should still net $100,000 to the entrepreneur for creating the business in the first place. If not earning this much the entrepreneur would be better off working on the development of another one million dollar value business.

Another way to look at the valuation method is to consider the $100,000 net income as the interest (or dividend) from investing one million dollars. This 10% rate of return per year is the minimum return to be demanded on invested risk capital. Venture capitalists often expect a higher rate, such as 25%, when investing in early stage enterprises. However, I use the guideline 10% for start-ups where I have an active involvement, and other financial rewards including consulting fees, bonuses, cash distributions and an ownership interest.

The creation of this amount of income is easier than you might think. It breaks down to $8,333 per month. Consider a real estate investor with a number of rental houses that on the average generate a cash flow of $83.33 per month after all costs including reserves for maintenance and replacement. If the investor acquires 12 houses (one per month) in a year the earnings will be $1,000 per month (12 x $83.33). To reach a valuation of one million dollars, this real estate business will need to acquire a hundred investment houses, each throwing off $83.33 per month or $100,000 per year.

That is a lot of houses! However the disciplined entrepreneur will find this achievable. Provided however that the entrepreneur builds a system which includes finders, negotiators, financing sources, renters, maintenance contractors, collectors, managers, real estate agents and bookkeepers.

The development of the real estate business *system* should be the primary task during the first year. Let me repeat this critically important concept. The first priority is to prepare and build the system. Only then does the entrepreneur focus on property acquisition.

Another real estate millionaire idea is for the entrepreneur to acquire only ten positive cash flow houses for an average $100,000 each. If positive cash flow is applied to the pay down of mortgages then the properties should be free and clear in 15 to 25 years. This system would generate a net worth of a million dollars, although taking twice as long as the other example. Note that as long as current tax laws stay in place there is the added advantage of deducting depreciation expense (a non-cash expense) in preparing annual tax returns. This will shelter some of the cash flow from income tax.

Yet another idea is to spend a year planning, developing and finding high margin wholesale products, and hiring a 12-man sales team to sell them. The objective would be to generate a minimum net profit of $1,000 per month per man. In total the team would produce $144,000 net income per year. The entrepreneur would then have the option to add a team manager for $44,000 per year. The net to the entrepreneur would be $100,000 per year, and the value of this cash flow would be $1,000,000 as an earnings stream.

The term *"being in business for yourself"* is a misnomer. If you are the sole practitioner then you have a job, not a business. You have simply swapped bosses to the person you see in the mirror each morning. Being self-employed, or in business for yourself, may give personal satisfaction and good earnings. In addition you may build up your net worth over time. *However, it is not a business!*

A business is not a one man band. It is a system that will continue to operate without you. This type of business can be sold as a system. A business that needs your attention all the time is an anchor. If you are chained to it, then it is the boss, not you.

On the other hand if you create a self-sustaining business system in one year, then next year you can build another one, and so on! Planned carefully and implemented consistently this method will build you a very substantial income and net worth. Self-sustaining businesses may be sold, franchised, left to heirs, or kept as cash generators that need little monitoring.

SUMMARY

Entrepreneurs frequently do not comprehend the power of building a system when developing their start-ups. Instead, they end up "buying a job for themselves." Time spent in planning a start-up should include some hard thinking on how to build a business system. This thought process should include how to locate and develop an executive who will manage the business in the entrepreneur's absence.

ACTION

Prepare a one page plan summary titled "How to build a business system not just a start-up – in 2000 hours."

Building a Business

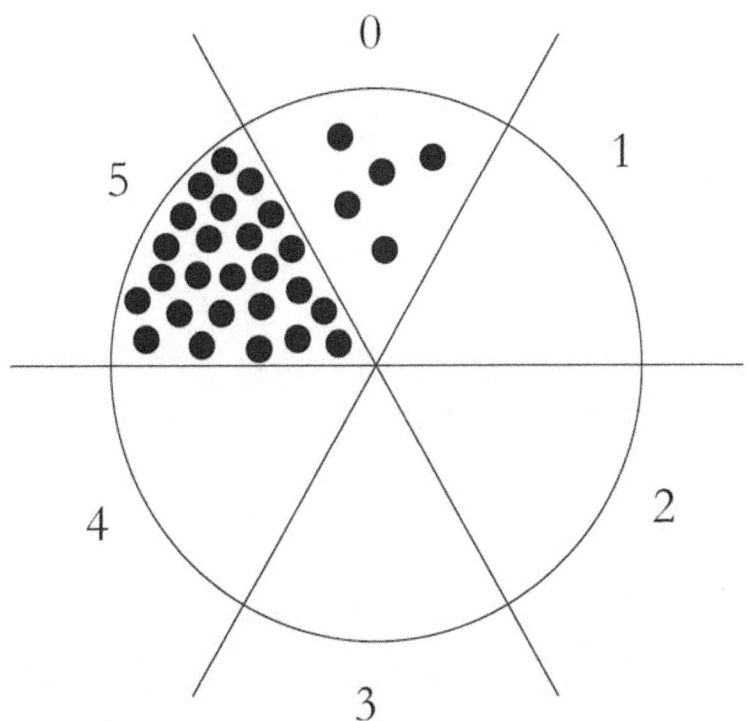

SCORING

Average score of my failures: 4.6
(I bought a lot of jobs for myself)

Average score of my successes: 2.0
(much better business systems development)

Your score is _____?

21

WHEN ENOUGH THINGS GO RIGHT

"Before everything else, getting ready is the secret of success."
— Henry Ford

While it's instructive to learn about situations in which mistakes were made and businesses failed, it is also instructive to look at a start-up where things were mainly done right and went right.

At the time I was living in Houston and holding monthly business meetings with my son in San Antonio. Mainly I drove, and if I set out early in the morning the sun would rise brightly in my rear view mirror. After a few miles of office buildings and shopping malls, the smell of gas permeated the air from the oil well pumps. Then came miles of horse and cattle ranches. Overall it was a long straight boring drive. On the way back I was often so tired that I would stop for a twenty minute power nap. There was one benefit which I often partook of; half way I would stop at a Dairy Queen and buy a mini Blizzard®.

The San Antonio office housed our wholesale business. After attending to administrative matters, we would adjourn to a Souper Salad restaurant. The waiters there knew us and would bring us a constant supply of diet coke. These meetings lasted two hours or more as we discussed the status of our businesses and investments. At one meeting my son brought up the idea of opening an auto sales and financing business. We agreed to research this idea.

The initial investigation took several months. This included market potential, competition, USP, site alternatives, legal requirements, forms, procedures, state and federal taxation, licensing, computer systems and financing. We consulted with industry experts and attended industry conferences, taking prodigious notes in the process. Many visits were made to local businesses in the same field. Several of these provided useful advice and operating information.

Research also included how to source inventory at auction and from individual wholesalers. In addition maintenance and reconditioning were studied, as was vehicle sales documentation, title processing and license tags.

The study of the auto financing side of the business received special attention. This critical part of the business includes loan underwriting, credit verification, loan servicing, insurance, claims processing, customer service, payment processing, and collateral repossession as necessary.

Several versions of the business plan were prepared. The financial pro-forma included a projection of the capital needed to reach break-even cash flow. This section of the plan was reworked multiple times as we gained more knowledge.

The equity investment required was substantial. To avoid diluting our ownership with third party investors we decided to self-fund the capital. I determined to 'bet the farm' by tapping into my real estate and stock market investments. The available capital came from prior successful start-ups and from many years of frugal savings.

In the final stages of planning we decided that an experienced operating partner was needed. Our new partner was a friend of my son who had many years of automobile sales and financing experience.

We launched the business from our existing wholesale parts office location in San Antonio. To do this we squeezed three more desks into a small executive office.

Our location in San Antonio was fortuitous in that only two competitors had any noticeable market share. In addition the economy in San Antonio had not been materially impacted by the financial crisis of 2007, and the subsequent downturn.

The first sales lot we leased was on an old highway centrally located for our target market. Our partner made the first wholesale purchases and stocked the lot. Gradually salesmen and mechanics were hired as the business grew. Procedures and forms were developed for the sales function and to document the loans. An industry computer system was purchased to automate the sales and loan servicing process. "Quick Books™" was adopted for our accounting and bookkeeping.

Our Unique Selling Proposition (USP) was to provide the customer with a reliable vehicle throughout the 36 month life of the average contract. A 100-point vehicle inspection program was introduced to ensure that vehicles were properly repaired and made ready for the customers.

Apart from providing the initial capital my involvement included bank presentations, planning, special assignments and accounting problem research.

Not every decision we made was for the best. Our first tax returns were prepared on a cash basis when they should have been on an accrual basis. Another mistake was that we did not consider an exit strategy, nor have a buy-sell agreement for the owners.

There were teething pains with the service department. Much of this was due to our lack of shop management and vehicle make-ready knowledge. None of us had served an apprenticeship in this side of our new business. We were 'green' and it showed.

However, the service function settled down, sales moved into high gear and the notes receivable portfolio grew rapidly. Significant learning was gained from industry conferences, local business groups, and "20 group" meetings of geographically separated dealers. These continue to provide an excellent sounding board and learning experience.

After two years in business we formed a finance company to acquire the growing portfolio of notes receivable. In the process, we met with a CPA with industry experience. He pointed out changes needed to our federal tax returns to correct a prior accountant's mistakes. This required that we file an amended IRS return and recognize additional income on our tax returns for the next four years.

The original forecast of the time and funding to achieve break-even proved to be substantially accurate. However, I pushed for the opening of a second lot to grow sales faster. My vision was to add one lot per year. However, like the World War II campaign in Holland, known as Market Garden, 'This was a bridge too far'.

We quickly appreciated that each new lot required almost as much new working capital as the first lot. To double sales and notes receivable one needed to buy twice the cars as well as replace those that were paid off. In addition cars damaged beyond repair were wholesales and also needed replacing.

This was a working capital problem as discussed in Chapter 9. We used profits, vendor's loans, personal credit cards, and we stretched our payment dates for accounts payable.

This was not enough, so I increased my loans to the business. I sourced this money by cashing in my retirement account, and by securing a 13% interest loan against other assets.

Though not long in business, we went after bank financing. With our prior planning experience, we made an effective presentation of our business and financial plan to the very sharp manager of a small local bank. She agreed to provide us with a loan that gave us breathing room. Later we financed the purchase of both sales lots with this bank. However to grow our portfolio further we needed a larger line of credit. Luckily a bank that specialized in our industry was looking for new borrowers. After careful due diligence that bank agreed to provide a substantial line of credit. In addition their covenants, reporting requirements and audits helped us maintain control over our growing notes receivable.

One of our strategic decisions was to lease space for our headquarters office away from our operating locations. With big dreams, we expected to grow quickly and therefore believed we would need to develop a centralized system with high quality executive management. However we would have had greater operational control had we operated from one of the sales lots from the beginning.

Now seven years later the business is profitable, and can sustain steady growth in receivables, with its current cash flow and loan agreements. We recently moved our headquarters to a new operating location which combines sales, service and administration as well. Future growth is possible based on a favorable economy and available financing. Our other two lots are now dedicated to customer vehicle repair, inventory acquisition and "get ready".

We did much right in this start-up. But, as discussed above, we made several mistakes as well. To a large extent this business was supported by the equity capital and experience acquired in prior start-ups. This success cannot be considered in isolation because it was the direct descendant of a lot of failures!

SUMMARY

Our car sales and financing business was built by avoiding most of the twenty failure factors (by scoring low). There was a strong emphasis on research, business planning, experienced partners, market selection and an established industry. Funding difficulties were experienced due to rapid growth. Errors were made in company formation and tax accounting. However, after seven years the business is profitable and growing steadily.

ACTION

Have you planned your start-up in as much detail as we did? Do you have enough relevant education and experience? Make sure you have enough working capital.

SCORING

Doing Things Right

The total score for this successful start-up was 28 out of 100. Had my research into failure factors been available at the time, we could probably have lowered this score still further.

22

OTHER FAILURE FACTORS AND CONCLUDING COMMENTS

HOME DISTRACTIONS

At least 34 million people work from home, full or part time. I am one of them. I have had a home office ever since I went into business for myself in 1981.

The setup cost is lower at home, so positive cash flow should occur earlier than in an outside office or plant. Savings include rent, furniture, telephone and other resources, all of which may be tax deductible. The home is a great place to test new business ideas.

Still, some people find that being productive in the home atmosphere is difficult. There are too many distractions like the TV, shopping list, honey 'do' lists and dogs barking. One distraction at my house is a very vocal cat named Alley. She stands at the end of the hallway and screams at me to let her out. Later, she meows at my window to come in. She is a frequent interruption that I acknowledge I have no control over.

In the home environment one must be especially disciplined to start work on time, day after day. I do not have a problem with starting work on time when working out of my home office. The problem is that the work is always there. Too often I find myself still in my home office at midnight and on the weekends. My need is to take more breaks and time off for exercise, family and relaxation.

The alternative to a home office is to rent space, perhaps in an executive office suite. The entrepreneur may find that going to work on time, working diligently through the day, and leaving work at a set time, is easier in this more formal situation. This depends on the individual.

Working at home may have drawbacks in terms of the image you present to customers and others. At home, pretending that you have a receptionist or an executive assistant, and are operating out of a professional office is difficult. The same goes for cell phone calls on the beach, or on the golf course.

Emergencies can occur at home that are completely unlike those occurring in a "normal" work environment. During one of my start-ups I was negotiating the purchase of an apartment building on my townhouse phone. Suddenly there were screams coming from my teenage daughter as she ran in the front door. I dropped the phone and ran into the hall. "What's wrong?" I called out, a very worried father. Sobbing, my daughter blurted out "The dog killed a rabbit." "Are you hurt?" I said. My distressed daughter continued in gasps. "I saw a rabbit... in a bush ... and pointed it out ... to the dog. I thought... he would be interested. But he bolted into the bush... grabbed the rabbit... and shook it to death." "Dogs do that!" I said in my least sympathetic, pragmatic manner. "

Later that night the realtor phoned back and the negotiation was finalized. Next day she and another agent brought the contract to the house for my signature. An important factor was that she agreed to carry her commission, through a note payable over five years to reduce the amount of cash needed to close. And that is how I bought my third apartment building.

An excellent book on this subject is *"Working from Home"* by Paul & Sarah Edwards.

MANAGEMENT SKILLS

Management experience in a large corporation did not prepare me for the range of duties and the hands-on nature of a start-up business. However, my corporate experience did give me an experience edge with lawyers, accountants, business planning, employee selection, training, and record keeping, all of which become increasingly useful and important as my businesses grew.

Relevant management experience for start-ups may be acquired in organizing and coordinating activities as wide ranging as caring for children, household management, committees, clubs and fundraising.

The management process in essence consists of the following:

1. Establish goals
2. Identify the steps to accomplish the goals
3. Assign duties and responsibilities for the steps
4. Measure the results
5. Decide if corrections or changes are needed
6. Establish new goals and continue the process in a circular fashion

TIME MANAGEMENT

Nearly everyone has a 'To Do List' written or unwritten, which is driven by the demands of everyday circumstances. The mother with a newborn infant must feed, change, bathe and wash the baby in a steady rotation. The business executive attends meetings, handles incoming documents and digital messages, makes speeches, fills in forms and strives to stay ahead of a deluge of information. These are simply the basic demands of the job and take up much of the day.

In reality, most of us have very little time to call our own. In those precious minutes we may pay attention to our top priority tasks. The priority tasks are determined as follows:

1. Write down twenty things you would like to achieve or do, in your lifetime.
2. Select five for action in the next five years.
3. Lay out the action steps you will take this year to progress towards your five year goals.
4. Review your annual plan and set up monthly action plans.
5. Refer to your monthly action plan while preparing a daily To Do List with five top priority items. This practice will put you in the successful minority who maintain and follow daily plans.
6. Whenever you have some time of your own look at your To Do List and work on the top priority items. Thus, whenever you have control of your time, you will be working towards the 'accomplishment of your life goals.
7. At the end of your work day prepare the next day's To Do List. This will ensure that you hit the ground running each morning.
8. Once a year review life goals, plans and priorities. Consider the progress you have made and

determine if changes are needed. Then review your five-year, one-year and monthly plans and revise as necessary. Your birthday is a good day for this review, as you reflect on the speed at which time goes by, and how you wish to spend the years remaining to you.

POOR QUALITY PERFORMANCE

The reliability of Japanese cars and products is generally accepted. The 2010 Toyota accelerator problem led to speculation that their quality was declining. The final report determined that the problem was customer-caused and not mechanical. However, the damage to the Toyota image shows the importance of attention to customer care.

Japanese product quality was developed over many years through programs such as *Zero Defects, Kaizen, Six Sigma and TQM*. Much of the effectiveness of these programs comes from orientating the entire management team and all other personnel to work to perfect customer care, and to develop perfect products. The entrepreneur must strive to emulate these examples. This is simply essential. Nothing else will do.

A few months ago, I received an attorney's letter announcing the planned foreclosure of one of my rental properties. Apparently there was an overdue Home Owners Association (HOA) bill. When I spoke to the president of my property management company he said: "Oh, yes. We get those all the time. They send the HOA invoice to the property address, and the tenants do not take any action. That is why we recommend that the owner be in direct contact with the HOA." The HOA made a small reduction for me, but the lawyer still wanted his cut. "Ouch", I thought – a $120 bill had grown to $2,500 with late fees, interest and the legal fees. This meant that the rental house had negative cash flow for the year.

The problem had arisen when the closing agent used the rental property address as my address rather than my home address. Of course it was also my mistake as I had not scrutinized the closing documents closely enough. When I checked my other rentals I found that another HOA invoice was in arrears and penalties and interest had accrued. The profit margin on rental properties is too thin for this type of mistake. My management company and I needed to pay closer attention to the details!

Accuracy and quality control pay for themselves. Entrepreneurs and their managers must pay strict attention to detail. Quality control and accuracy is a company-wide objective starting from the top down. The very survival of the business is at stake.

When mistakes occur, the true cause must be identified, and action taken to minimize recurrence. This action may require employee re-training, and, changes in procedures and forms.

FRANCHISES

The franchise industry is promoted as one of the safest and best ways to success in your own business. However an article in Franchising World by Darrell Johnson and John Reynolds tells a different story. They found that from 2001 to 2006 the average charge off rate was 6.5% for franchise loans and 5.9% for comparable non-franchise loans made under the SBA's 7(a) and 504 loan programs. Failure rates vary from none to 69% in a brand analysis of SBA data for the period 2000 to 2007. This reference was posted by the web site bluemaumau.org in December 2008.

Due diligence and preparation are as important in buying a franchise as in any other start-up. Interestingly, some well-known brands have a high failure rate including Aamco Transmissions, Marble Slab Creamery, Petland, Carvel, Blimpie and Quiznos. On the other hand, Snap-On Tools, 7-Eleven and Aaron's had low failure rates according to J.J. Coloa in a Forbes article noted on msnbc.msn.com, February 2012.

The closest I came to buying a franchise was in the energy conservation field in England. The package included training, sales advice and engineering support. My job was to find clients through cold calling. Then, the franchising company arranged for an engineer to visit the plant or office, and conduct a study. I made good money in this business, but I hated the cold calling. So I closed it down after a year and moved on to other ventures.

POSITIVE RESULTS

Failing forward is a life affirming and beneficial approach to eventual achievement. Babe Ruth struck out frequently on the way to a magnificent record accomplished without the benefit of performance enhancing drugs – actually, he looks a little pudgy in the old newsreels!

Napoleon Hill, author of *Think and Grow Rich* examined the stupendous success of Andrew Carnegie, Thomas Edison and Henry Ford and concluded that "Patience, persistence and perspiration make an unbeatable combination for success." Edison in particular, is known to have tested and failed, again and again, before proving that carbon filament was the thing for the electric light bulb. Mind you, he had a lot of research assistants by that time!

Start-up entrepreneurs must keep going through thick and thin. In *212°: The Extra Degree* authors Parker and Anderson note that water boils and turns into steam only from the last degree of heat. That degree sits on top of 211° degrees of effort. Yet at 212° degrees high pressure steam will drive a locomotive. So keep going!

With 25 failures out of 30 "attempts at bat," my failure rate was 83% and my success rate was 17%. So the best advice I can give an entrepreneur is to learn from my mistakes, as well as my successes. That way the entrepreneur may achieve a higher success rate – as indeed I expect to myself in the future.

In conclusion, well thought-out business ideas for a start-up, still involve daring and risk. Most start-ups end in failure with loss of time and money. The entrepreneur whose start-up achieves lasting success, with equity buildup, profits and strong positive cash flow, is worthy of applause and recognition.

If, by the greatest of good fortune and effective effort, your enterprise is a success - then you will be in a position to agree with me that "One non-failing start-up is enough…for any one…and for a lifetime." What is more - you may firmly claim: "I have learned my trade. I am *AN ENTREPRENEUR*."

Appendix

FAILURE SCORING MODEL

THE SUCCESSES

FACTORS	1 Bootstrap Multi-Units	2 Land & Office Developer	3 GP Multi-Units	4 Financial Consultant	5 Auto Financing
1 Inadequate Desire and Motivation	0	0	0	0	0
2 Negative Cash Flow	3	3	3	0	0
3 The Wrong Industries	3	0	0	0	0
4 Did Not Serve an Apprenticeship in Field	0	5	0	3	5
5 The Wrong Partners	0	0	0	0	0
6 Lack of Small Business Executive Experience	0	0	0	0	5
7 Physical, Mental or Emotional Weakness	0	0	0	0	3
8 Bad Legal and Accounting Advice	0	0	1	0	4
9 Shortage of Working Capital	0	3	0	3	0
10 Lack of Respect for Planning	5	0	3	5	0
11 Non-Use of Project Planning and Control	3	0	3	0	3
12 Weak USP, Sales and Marketing	5	0	3	3	0
13 Lack of Accounting Knowledge	0	0	3	0	0
14 Wrong Hires and Failing to Fire Them	0	3	3	0	3
15 Negative Economy	0	5	2	0	0
16 Lack of Relevant Education	0	5	3	3	5
17 Incompetent or Unused Directors/Advisors	5	0	3	5	0
18 Not Sticking to One Business	5	0	3	0	0
19 Bad Luck and Black Swan Events	0	5	0	3	0
20 Not Building a Sustainable Business System	5	0	0	5	0
Total Score out of Maximum 100	**34**	**29**	**30**	**30**	**28**

FAILURE SCORING MODEL

THE FAILURES

FACTORS	6 Trading Precious Metals	7 Limited Partnerships	8 Single Family Rentals	9 Multi-Level Mktg	10 Real Estate Broker
1 Inadequate Desire and Motivation	5	3	4	5	4
2 Negative Cash Flow	0	5	3	3	3
3 The Wrong Industries	5	3	3	5	3
4 Did Not Serve an Apprenticeship in Field	5	5	3	5	5
5 The Wrong Partners	0	5	0	0	0
6 Lack of Small Business Executive Experience	0	5	0	5	5
7 Physical, Mental or Emotional Weakness	5	0	0	5	3
8 Bad Legal and Accounting Advice	0	0	5	0	0
9 Shortage of Working Capital	0	5	0	0	0
10 Lack of Respect for Planning	5	5	5	5	5
11 Non-Use of Project Planning and Control	5	5	5	5	5
12 Weak USP, Sales and Marketing	5	5	5	5	5
13 Lack of Accounting Knowledge	0	5	3	3	3
14 Wrong Hires and Failing to Fire Them	0	0	0	0	0
15 Negative Economy	5	5	5	2	3
16 Lack of Relevant Education	5	5	5	5	5
17 Incompetent or Unused Directors/Advisors	5	5	5	5	5
18 Not Sticking to One Business	5	5	5	5	5
19 Bad Luck and Black Swan Events	0	3	3	0	0
20 Not Building a Sustainable Business System	5	5	5	5	5
Total Score out of Maximum 100	**55**	**79**	**64**	**68**	**64**

FAILURE SCORING MODEL

THE FAILURES

FACTORS	11 Business Consulting Company	12 New Car Dealer	13 Temporary Help	14 Energy Consultant	15 Web Site Developer
1 Inadequate Desire and Motivation	0	0	5	5	4
2 Negative Cash Flow	0	5	5	3	5
3 The Wrong Industries	0	3	3	3	5
4 Did Not Serve an Apprenticeship in Field	5	5	5	5	5
5 The Wrong Partners	5	5	5	0	5
6 Lack of Small Business Executive Experience	3	5	5	0	5
7 Physical, Mental or Emotional Weakness	0	5	5	5	5
8 Bad Legal and Accounting Advice	0	5	5	0	0
9 Shortage of Working Capital	5	5	5	5	3
10 Lack of Respect for Planning	5	5	5	5	5
11 Non-Use of Project Planning and Control	5	5	5	3	5
12 Weak USP, Sales and Marketing	5	5	5	5	5
13 Lack of Accounting Knowledge	0	5	5	3	5
14 Wrong Hires and Failing to Fire Them	0	5	5	3	3
15 Negative Economy	5	0	5	0	0
16 Lack of Relevant Education	3	5	5	5	5
17 Incompetent or Unused Directors/Advisors	5	5	5	5	5
18 Not Sticking to One Business	5	5	5	5	5
19 Bad Luck and Black Swan Events	0	5	3	0	0
20 Not Building a Sustainable Business System	5	5	5	5	5
Total Score out of Maximum 100	56	88	96	62	80

FAILURE SCORING MODEL

THE FAILURES

FACTORS	16 General Contractor	17 Tanning Booths	18 Fasteners	19 Parts Distributor	20 Electrical Contractor
1 Inadequate Desire and Motivation	5	5	3	3	3
2 Negative Cash Flow	5	5	3	3	5
3 The Wrong Industries	0	5	0	0	4
4 Did Not Serve an Apprenticeship in Field	5	5	5	5	5
5 The Wrong Partners	5	5	5	0	5
6 Lack of Small Business Executive Experience	5	5	5	5	3
7 Physical, Mental or Emotional Weakness	5	5	3	3	0
8 Bad Legal and Accounting Advice	5	0	3	3	3
9 Shortage of Working Capital	5	5	3	0	5
10 Lack of Respect for Planning	5	5	5	5	5
11 Non-Use of Project Planning and Control	5	5	5	5	5
12 Weak USP, Sales and Marketing	5	5	5	5	5
13 Lack of Accounting Knowledge	5	5	5	5	2
14 Wrong Hires and Failing to Fire Them	5	5	3	5	5
15 Negative Economy	0	0	3	3	5
16 Lack of Relevant Education	5	5	5	5	5
17 Incompetent or Unused Directors/Advisors	5	5	5	5	3
18 Not Sticking to One Business	5	5	5	5	5
19 Bad Luck and Black Swan Events	5	5	0	0	5
20 Not Building a Sustainable Business System	5	5	5	0	5
Total Score out of Maximum 100	**90**	**90**	**76**	**65**	**83**

FAILURE SCORING MODEL.

THE FAILURES

FACTORS	21 Stock Market Investor	22 Phlebotomy	23 Used Cars Sales	24 Antique Car Restorer	25 Spring Water Distributor
1 Inadequate Desire and Motivation	0	5	5	5	5
2 Negative Cash Flow	0	5	5	5	5
3 The Wrong Industries	5	5	0	0	0
4 Did Not Serve an Apprenticeship in Field	5	5	5	5	5
5 The Wrong Partners	5	5	5	0	5
6 Lack of Small Business Executive Experience	0	5	5	5	5
7 Physical, Mental or Emotional Weakness	0	5	5	5	5
8 Bad Legal and Accounting Advice	5	5	5	5	5
9 Shortage of Working Capital	5	5	5	5	5
10 Lack of Respect for Planning	5	5	5	5	5
11 Non-Use of Project Planning and Control	5	5	5	5	5
12 Weak USP, Sales and Marketing	5	5	5	5	5
13 Lack of Accounting Knowledge	0	5	5	5	5
14 Wrong Hires and Failing to Fire Them	5	3	5	3	5
15 Negative Economy	5	3	5	5	5
16 Lack of Relevant Education	5	5	5	5	5
17 Incompetent or Unused Directors/Advisors	5	5	5	5	5
18 Not Sticking to One Business	5	5	5	5	5
19 Bad Luck and Black Swan Events	5	0	5	5	5
20 Not Building a Sustainable Business System	5	5	5	5	5
Total Score out of Maximum 100	**75**	**91**	**95**	**88**	**95**

FAILURE SCORING MODEL

THE FAILURES

	FACTORS	26 Writer	27 Importer	28 Foreclosure Investment	29 Aerial Photography	30 Immigration Consultant
1	Inadequate Desire and Motivation	0	5	4	5	5
2	Negative Cash Flow	5	5	5	5	5
3	The Wrong Industries	5	0	0	3	3
4	Did Not Serve an Apprenticeship in Field	5	5	5	5	5
5	The Wrong Partners	5	5	0	5	5
6	Lack of Small Business Executive Experience	0	5	5	5	5
7	Physical, Mental or Emotional Weakness	0	5	5	5	5
8	Bad Legal and Accounting Advice	0	5	5	0	5
9	Shortage of Working Capital	5	5	5	3	3
10	Lack of Respect for Planning	5	5	5	5	5
11	Non-Use of Project Planning and Control	5	5	3	5	5
12	Weak USP, Sales and Marketing	5	5	5	5	5
13	Lack of Accounting Knowledge	0	3	5	0	5
14	Wrong Hires and Failing to Fire Them	5	0	5	0	0
15	Negative Economy	0	0	0	0	0
16	Lack of Relevant Education	5	5	5	5	5
17	Incompetent or Unused Directors/Advisors	5	5	5	5	5
18	Not Sticking to One Business	5	5	5	5	5
19	Bad Luck and Black Swan Events	5	0	0	5	0
20	Not Building a Sustainable Business System	0	5	5	5	5
	Total Score out of Maximum 100	65	78	77	76	81

FAILURE SCORING MODEL

Factor Summary

FACTORS	Failures Average Score	Successes Average Score	Your Score
Inadequate Desire and Motivation	3.7	0.0	
Negative Cash Flow	3.9	1.8	
The Wrong Industries	2.5	0.6	
Did Not Serve an Apprenticeship in Field	4.9	2.6	
The Wrong Partners	3.4	0.0	
Lack of Small Business Executive Experience	3.8	1.0	
Physical, Mental or Emotional Weakness	3.6	0.6	
Bad Legal and Accounting Advice	2.8	1.0	
Shortage of Working Capital	3.7	1.2	
Lack of Respect for Planning	5.0	2.6	
Non-Use of Project Planning and Control	4.8	1.8	
Weak USP, Sales and Marketing	5.0	2.2	
Lack of Accounting Knowledge	3.5	0.6	
Wrong Hires and Failing to Fire Them	2.7	1.8	
Negative Economy	2.4	1.4	
Lack of Relevant Education	4.9	3.2	
Incompetent or Unused Directors/Advisors	4.9	2.6	
Not Sticking to One Business	5.0	1.6	
Bad Luck and Black Swan Events	2.4	1.6	
Not Building a Sustainable Business System	4.6	2.0	
Total Average Score	**77.5**	**30.2**	

APPENDIX

FAILURE SCORING MODEL
Company Summary

Business #	Successes	Scores	Years	Type
1	Bootstrap Multi-Units	34	7	Business
2	Land & Office Developer	29	20	Business
3	General Partner Multi-Units	30	15	Business
4	Financial Consultant	30	30	Self Employment
5	Auto Financing	28	6	Business
	Average Score of 5 Successes	**30**	**16**	

Business #	Failures	Scores	Years	Type
6	Trading Precious Metals	55	1	Self Employment
7	Limited Partnerships	79	4	Business
8	Single Family Rentals	64	10	Business
9	Multi-Level Marketing	68	5	Self Employment
10	Real Estate Broker	64	5	Self Employment
11	Business Consulting Company	56	2	Business
12	New Car Dealer	88	1	Business
13	Temporary Help	96	1	Business
14	Energy Consulting	62	1	Business
15	Web Site Developer	80	2	Business
16	General Contractor	90	1	Business
17	Tanning Booths	90	2	Business
18	Fasteners	76	5	Business
19	Parts Distributor	65	10	Business
20	Electrical Contractor	83	3	Business
21	Stock Market Investor	75	30	Self Employment
22	Phelbotomy	91	4	Business
23	Used Cars Sales	95	1	Business
24	Antique Car Restorer	88	1	Self Employment
25	Spring Water Distributor	95	1	Business
26	Writer	65	3	Self Employment
27	Importer	78	1	Self Employment
28	Foreclosure Investment	77	1	Self Employment
29	Aerial Photography	76	1	Business
30	Immigration Consultant	81	1	Business
	Average Score of 25 Failures	**77**	**4**	

BIBLIOGRAPHY

Abraham, Jay. *Your Marketing Genius at Work*. Abraham
Publishing Group, 1986.

Allen, Robert G. *Nothing Down: How to Buy Real Estate
with Little or No Money Down*. New York: Simon &
Schuster, 1980.

Bick, Julie. *All I Really Need to Know in Business I Learned at
Microsoft: Insider Strategies to Help You Succeed*. New York:
Pocket Books, 1997.

Blechman and Levinson. *Guerrilla Financing: Alternative
Techniques to Finance Any Small Business*. Boston:
Houghton Mifflin, 1991.

Corman, Joel and Lussier, Robert N. *Small Business
Management: A Planning Approach*. U.S.A.: Irwin, 1996.

Drucker, Peter. *Management: Tasks, Responsibilities, Practices*.
New York: Harper & Row, 1985.

Edwards, Paul and Sarah. *Working from Home*. New York:
G.P. Putnam's Sons, 1994.

Flyvbjerg, Holm and Buhl. *How Common and How Large
are Cost Overruns in Transport Infrastructure Projects?*
Transport Reviews: Taylor & Francis, 2003.

Graham, Benjamin. *The Intelligent Investor*. New York:
Harper & Brothers, 1949.

Graham, Benjamin and Dodd, David L. *Security Analysis*.
New York: McGraw-Hill, 1934.

Hansen, Mark V. and Allen, Robert G. *The One Minute
Millionaire*. New York: Harmony Books, 2002.

Hill, Napoleon. *Think and Grow Rich*. Meridian, Conn.:
Ralston Society, 1937.

Knaup, Amy E and Piazza Merissa C. *Business Employment*

Dynamics data: survival and longevity. Monthly Labor Review: U.S. Bureau of Labor Statistics, 2007.

Machiavelli, Niccolò. *The Prince.* Florence, 1532.

Mortensen, Kurt W. *Maximum Influence: The 12 Universal Laws of Power Persuasion.* New York: Amacon, 2004.

Parker, Sam and Anderson, Mac. *212°: The Extra Degree.* Aurora, Illinois: Simple Truths, 2006.

Peale, Norman Vincent. *The Amazing Results of Positive Thinking.* New York: Simon & Schuster, 1952.

Perot, Ross. *My Life and the Principles of Success.* Ottawa: Summit Group, 1996.

Peter, Lawrence and Hull, Raymond. *The Peter Principle: Why Things Always Go Wrong.* New York: William Morrow, 1969.

Robbins, Anthony. *Awaken the Giant Within: How to Take Immediate Control of Your Mental, Emotional, Physical & Financial Destiny.* New York: Simon & Schuster, 1992.

Robinette, Scott and Brand, Claire with Lenz, Vicki. *Emotion Marketing: The Hallmark Way of Winning Customers for Life.* New York: McGraw-Hill, 2001.

Shane, Scott. *Small Business Failure Rates by Industry: The Real Numbers.* Small Business Trends, 2012.

Taleb, Nassim. *The Black Swan: The Impact of the Highly Improbable.* New York: Random House, 2007.

Townsend Robert. *Up the Organization.* London: Michael Joseph Ltd, 1970.

Welch, Jack and Byrne, John A. *Jack Straight from the Gut.* New York: Warner Books, 2001.

ABOUT THE AUTHOR

John Charman was born in England and earned a B.Sc. Economics degree at the London School of Economics. He immigrated to the United States and became a U.S. citizen. Working in the corporate world he achieved the level of Vice President and Controller in a Fortune 500 company. At the peak of his career he stepped out, of his own volition, to pursue a lifelong dream to run his own business. As a beginning entrepreneur, he found his skill set was inadequate for the task of building a sustainable business and he had many failures before he achieved success. In total he has started 30 businesses of which 5 he considers to have been really successful. In the school of hard knocks John has developed a set of twenty factors which are essential for the development of a successful start-up. He stresses the importance of building a sustainable business system rather than just being self-employed. A sustainable system will continue to operate in the absence of the entrepreneur, and, may be sold or gifted as an ongoing valuable system. Living in San Antonio with his wife Maria, John has three successful children and three lovely granddaughters. His hobbies include international travel, live theater, antique books, the study of finance and economics, and, training for and completing triathlons. He remains active in a number of businesses.

Index